M000303698

FROM THE HEART OF A LION

לב אריה

FROM THE
HEART
of a
LION

Lev Aryeh on *Sefer Bereishis*

Rabbi Aryeh Cohen

Penina Press
Jerusalem ◆ New York

In honor of the bar mitzvah
of
SHMUEL YAAKOV COHEN

In memory of our beloved parents

YISSACHAR DOV (BERNARD)
& MIRIAM SELTZER

Debbie and David Seltzer & Family

In memory of our beloved fathers

AVRAHAM YEHUDAH TISSER
Who rose from the ashes of the Shoah
to build our family

and

Rav NASSAN GOODMAN

Esther and Nachman Goodman & Family

Contents

Acknowledgements

THE FIRST WORDS SPOKEN by every Jew upon awakening are an expression of gratitude. We arise from our slumber and pronounce the words *modeh ani,* literally, "thanks I give." We immediately show our appreciation to *Hashem* for gifting us with another day in this world. This *teffila* could have been re-arranged to have stated more simply *ani modeh*, "I give thanks," but *Chazal* desired to impress upon every *Yid* the importance of selfless gratitude. So they ingeniously codified the very first word out of every Jew's mouth would be "thank" rather than "I."

At the very essence of Judaism is that we all understand the appreciation owed to all that help us in any way. This is why we are called *Yehudim*. The root of this word is *hod*, to give thanks. Our foundation as a nation is based on the principle of giving thanks to *Hashem* and all who are there for us in our daily lives. There is no question that to acknowledge those who have helped inspire and create this *sefer* is the only proper place to begin.

The truth is that it would be impossible to name each person that owns a piece of this *sefer*. At my son Shmuel's *upsherin,* I explained the thought underlying the common *minhag* to allow all guests who are present to snip some hair. An *upsherin* is a celebration of the initial teaching of a child the rights from the wrongs. By cutting the hair we are teaching the child that no longer can life be free and wild. He has entered into the world of *chinuch* and it is time to begin to grow up. It is not merely the Rebbe in yeshiva or a parent in the home that has a monopoly on the *chinuch* of a child, but every friend or family member that the child comes in contact with has an effect on his upbringing. Every person at the *upsherin* must realize that they have an obligation to help in the proper *chinuch* of the child and therefore every person shares in the cutting of the hair.

This very much captures how I feel towards all of the special people in my life with whom I have merited special relationships. Whether a family member, friend, *Rebbe* or *talmid*, they have all helped mold me into who I am. The Torah in this *sefer* is an expression of my essence and therefore you all have a part in it. Each and every one of you deserves a personal thank you and I hope you feel my appreciation.

At the same time I would be remiss if I did not single out a few people who absolutely require an individual thank you.

There are a few individuals in one's life that feel more like family than friends. Debbie and David Seltzer and Esther and Nachman Goodman have been so much more than friends over the past few years. In ways that I can not express on these pages, they have been by my side always. To have these *gedolim* in *chessed* as the sponsors of this *sefer* is a true *zechus. Bezras Hashem* this should be a *zchus* for only *simcha* and *bracha* from their special families, from which some of my most special of *talmidim* come.

To my holy *Rabbeim,* to whom I truly owe not only my *Olam Habbah*, but my *Olam Hazeh* as well. It is the foundation they laid that supports all the Torah in these pages. Rav Yitzchak Cohen at a young age taught me what it means to have passion in *Avodas Hashem*. Rav Yisrael Kaminetsky believed in me as a confused teenager and continued to believe in me as a very young *mechanech*. My life as an *eved Hashem* was not only molded by Rabbi Kaminetsky as a mentor, but also as the *Menahel* of DRS, I am forever indebted to him for extending to me the opportunity to do what I love. Every drop of Torah I learn on some level is shared with Rav Mendel Blachman. I learned how to learn Torah from Rav Blachman and continue to learn how to live Torah from Rav Blachman until this very day. From Rav Yaakov Nueberger I have learned to balance the sensitivities of every situation in life with our holy Torah. The synthesis of Rav Neuberger's love of Torah and empathy towards all people is an inspiration and model I try to emulate. The Ostrov-Kaloshiner Rebbe, Harav Dovid Spiegel, has been my Rav for the past 8 years and has taught me that one can be an *eved Hashem* both *bepnimius* and *chitzonius* even in *chutz laaretz*. Finally I have the *zchus* to call Harav Nosson Tzvi Finkel *ztz"l* my Rebbe. In my life I knew nobody who was more inspiring. I deeply cherish the relationship we had. I had the privilege to be close to the greatest role model in the world.

There are a few people without whom this *sefer* could never have actually become a reality. Dr. Shlomo Koyfman is an inspiration to anyone who knows him, regarding what it means to be both a *ben Torah* as well as a *baal habayis*. For the past 18 years Shlomo has been my best friend and *chavrusa,* and there was nobody else that I would have wanted to help edit my Torah. Rabbi Natan Farber is a quintessential example of what a *talmid chaver* should be. Natan, one of my earliest *talmidim* who is now a colleague, was a tremendous help in many aspects of this *sefer*, especially with designing the beautiful cover. Who says you can't judge a book by its cover?

My beautiful children Shmuel Yaakov, Neshama Elianna, Eliora Malka, Nesya Tehilla, and Uriel Nosson Tzvi are the light of my life. Even on days when I am faced with dealing with very difficult *tzoros* in *Klal Yisael*, I come home and view one of your smiles and instantly my world is all good. Don't ever forget that you are my most precious *talmidim* as well. If the only ones who learn this *sefer* are you then it was all worth it.

Acharon acharon chaviv, my angelic *eishes chayil,* Shaindel Rivkah. I call her angelic as it is not possible for a human to accomplish all that she does. My wife is truly my foundation and the source of my blood flow. Anything that I have accomplished in my life and especially my life as a Rebbi is because of her *messiras nefesh.* I could say to all my *talmidim,* "*Sheli Veshelachem Shela hi.*" The *sefer* that flowed from my years of sharing Torah with my *talmidim* is therefore not mine, but hers.

Introduction

THERE IS ONE GROUP of individuals who are clearly omitted from the previous acknowledgements section. My precious students have inspired me to learn Torah in deeper ways and achieve levels I never could have dreamed possible. Every time I learn a beautiful piece of Torah or have the fortune to be *mechadesh* a new idea, my immediate thought is "I can't wait to share this treat with my *talmidim*." My *talmidim* have urged me for years to publish these *shiurim* in a *sefer* for others to learn from, and to have available a constant reference. My strongest motivation came from the *talmidim* of the Thursday night *shiur* that takes place in our home. Many of the ideas shared in this *sefer* came to fruition in the context of that special *shiur*, which I truly cherish every week. As *chazal* has taught us, *metalmidei yoser mekulam*.[1] Unquestionably, whatever I have achieved in learning in my life has been greatly enhanced by my amazing *talmidim*.

Being that there are never enough hours in the day, this dream of my *talmidim* took many years to materialize. It was the upcoming Bar Mitzvah of my *bechor* Shmuel Yaakov, that

---

1. *Taanis* 7a.

was the final impetus to bring it to reality. I decided that there was no better gift to present to my son as he enters into the world of Torah and *mitzvos* as a *bar chiyuva,* than my very own *Sefer Hachinuch* for him. The Torah and stories shared in this *sefer* will *Bezras Hashem* be etched on his heart as a *sefer* of guidance and inspiration.

Despite the prodding from my students and the approaching deadline of my son's Bar Mitzvah, two obstacles remained that I had to overcome. Firstly, I felt that my personal Torah and inspiration is absorbed exponentially more powerfully when heard in person than read in written form. When trying to bring out the beauty of a *parsha* and use it to inspire another Jew, the heart within the Torah must be felt. That is truly so much harder to do if you are not looking into someone's eyes and opening your heart with one's tone of voice. This is a sentiment shared by Rav Shneur Zalman of Liadi as he explains in the introduction to his *sefer Tanya* when he discloses his own hesitancy in writing the *sefer.* My second, most significant hesitation was based on my own doubts about being worthy to proceed. Who am I to write a *sefer*? What Torah do I really have to add to our great *Tzaddikim's* works?

To answer my first dilemma I came across a beautiful teaching of Rav Akiva Eiger. The Shulchan Aruch[2] explains that prior to writing down Torah one would need to first make *Birchas Hatorah.* In the very next *halacha*[3] Rav Yosef Karo states that one who plans on thinking about Torah does not need to first recite a Bracha. What is the difference between writing and thinking? Rav Akiva Eiger[4] explains that the main *kiyum*

---

2. *Orach Chaim, siman 47, seif 3.*
3. Ibid., *seif 4.*
4. *Shaalos Vetshuvos Rabbi Akiva Eiger, Orach Chaim 27.*

of the mitzvah of *Limud Hatorah* is to teach *Torah*. This is clear from the laws of *Talmud Torah* codified in the Rambam[5] and implied by the *pasukim* themselves from which the *mitzvah* is derived. One cannot teach Torah by merely thinking about the words, rather they must be articulated. Recording one's Torah in writing can still be a great source of teaching. For this reason, before writing Torah, a *Bracha* is required.

Although in a perfect world, the effect of inspirational Torah is strongest when delivered personally from *Rebbi* to *talmid*, writing a *sefer* will allow this Torah to be taught to many people whom I otherwise would never have had the opportunity to reach. If even one person finds inspiration in the words within this *sefer*, it is surely all worth it.

As far as my second trepidation in writing this *sefer*, I really never came upon a great resolution. I am comforted to some extent from the words of the *Tanya* who explains[6] that Torah can only be deeply understood by those who live in a very physical and materialistic world. Only via breaking the temptations of this world does one have the privilege to break through into the *pnimiyus* of Torah. Perhaps, as the world becomes more and more steeped in materialism and temptation, there are opportunities to see depth in Torah which may never have been considered before. While I still feel unworthy, I personally have derived tremendous pleasure and been inspired by the Torah I have learned and included in the *sefer*, and hopefully there are others who will find the same.

This *sefer* includes an essay on every *parsha* in *Sefer Bereishis*. Each *maamar* on every *parsha* was written straight from my heart. Each Torah was one that I connected to intellectually

---

5. *Hilchos Talmud Torah, Perek 1, Laws 1:2.*
6. Igros Hakodesh 26.

and emotionally, and I pray that all learners will feel the same. Every source quoted is footnoted so that all can learn the source on their own.

Many people like to say that The Baal Shem Tov introduced the idea to the world to teach Torah with the usage of stories. The truth is The Ribbono Shel Olam is the greatest story teller, and already taught us the power of a story in the beginning of His Torah, as most of *Sefer Bereishis* is comprised of stories. I therefore decided to end each essay with a personal story from my own life.

The other reason I decided to conclude each piece with a story in itself derives from a story I once heard from my Rebbi, Harav Nosson Tzvi Finkel *ztz"l*. Rav Nosson Tzvi was once approached by a widow who was crying bitter tears of loneliness at the loss of her husband of fifty years. She complained that she didn't feel that she could go on in such a lonely state. Rav Nosson Tzvi told her that she should go purchase a small pad and pen to carry with her always. Anytime she experienced the feeling that *Hashem* was by her side, he instructed her to write it in her notepad. Whether in a revealed state or more hidden, every recognition of Hashem's presence in her life should be recorded. During her loneliest moments, he suggested that she open her pad and start reading. Hashem is always by your side and therefore there is no place for loneliness.

The stories of my life have similarly helped build my *emunah* that *Hashem* is by my side at every moment, and I hope this will help inspire others to feel the same.

Baruch Shehechiyunu Vekimunu Vehigiyunu Lazman Hazeh!!
Hodu L'Hashem Ki Tov Ki Laolam Chasdo!!

— ARYEH YEHUDA COHEN
Lag B'omer, 5774

Parshas Bereishis

To Brighten the World With the *Ohr* of Torah

בראשית ברא א־להים את השמים ואת הארץ: והארץ היתה תהו
ובהו וחשך על־פני תהום ורוח א־להים מרחפת על־פני המים: ויאמר
א־להים יהי אור ויהי־אור[1]

*In the beginning Hashem created the heavens and the earth.
The earth was desolate and darkness was on the surface of
the deep, and the spirit of Hashem hovered above the water.
Hashem said "Let there be light." There was light.*

I N L I F E T H E R E A R E moments of clarity and moments of
darkness. There are times when we understand all that is oc-
curring in our life and we are full of happiness, and other times
of bleak confusion that leaves a person in a state of sadness or
even depression. Every one of us is surely searching for a life of
joy that is void of confusion. As our Sages tell us, *"Ein simcha
kehataras safeik."* There is no greater joy than the resolution of
doubt. The problem that remains is how to achieve this joy of
clarity and remove all of our doubts.

There is no question that the opening words of the holy
Torah, the opening words that *Hashem* chose to share with

---

1. *Bereishis, perek* 1, *pasukim* 1–3

His nation, are words full of inspiration, meaning and crucial life lessons. They may even hint at the essential character of the world in which we live. From the simple reading of these first three *pasukim* of the Torah we understand that the world we live in at its core is full of darkness and confusion. Light is an entity that was subsequently created to brighten existence. This is understood by the mere fact that darkness was never created, but existed at the inception of Creation. The *Nesivos Shalom*[2] explains that the Hebrew word for the world, *olam*, also means to be hidden. *Hashem* has been *metzamtzaim*[3] himself and is hidden in this world leaving it essentially in the dark. After describing this dark essential nature of the world, we find *Hashem* creating light as a clear contrast to this original darkness.

Rashi on the very next verse suggests that this *Ohr*, this light, is not a physical light, but a spiritual radiance that was hidden away soon after creation.[4] Although explained by *Rashi* as an *Aggadic* interpretation, this elucidation I believe can also be the basic explanation of this *Ohr*. The physical light that we benefit from today stems from our luminaries created on the fourth day as is explained explicitly in *pasukim* 16 and 17. The purpose of the creation of luminaries was to bring physical light to the world and introduce the cycle of day and night, which clearly did not previously exist. The light created on the first day of creation, therefore must not relate to physical light, but rather provides a spiritual light to help us navigate and overcome the natural darkness of this world. The world can often lead one

---

2. *Nesevei Torah, maamar* 1

3. *Tzimtzum* is the Kabbalistic term used to describe the idea that *Hashem* has chosen to minimize himself in order to be present in a hidden nature in our world.

4. *Rashi Bereishis, Perek* 1, *Pasuk* 4

astray to follow empty goals and aspirations full of darkness fueled by temptation and laziness. Spiritual light is our guide to give clarity to our individual worlds.

However, the problem remains: If this *Ohr* is crucial to our spiritual survival and success in this world, why would *Hashem* place it away into hiding? *Rashi* quoting the *Gemara* in *Chagigah*[5] explains that this light could not be left open and accessible for anyone to grab, as the wicked would be able to seize it as well. Sinful individuals have no rights to connect to this *Ohr* and therefore it was placed into *genizah*.[6]

What path is then left for those of us who want and need this light to understand how to elevate the beautiful world in which we live? Is our ability to view the world with clarity impossible now that this *Ohr Haganuz* has been hidden?

The *Midresh Tanchuma*[7] explains that the light of the first day of creation has been stored away for those who toil in *Torah Shebaal Peh*, the oral Torah. The *Ohr* can be found and used within the holy Torah. When one studies Torah with toil he can become one with this *Ohr* and see the world with clarity. Without Torah, we revert back to being spiritually blind, observing a world full of confusion and darkness.

Now we *understand* the following *Gemara* in *Shabbos*[8]

דאמר ריש לקיש: מאי דכתיב ויהי ערב ויהי בקר יום הששי, ה"א יתירה למה לי? מלמד שהתנה הקדוש ברוך הוא עם מעשה בראשית, ואמר להם: אם ישראל מקבלים התורה – אתם מתקיימין, ואם לאו אני מחזיר אתכם לתוהו ובוהו.

5. *Chagigah 12a.*
6. Hidden away.
7. *Midrash Tanchuma, Parshas Noach 3.*
8. *Shabbos 88a.*

> *Reish Lakish said "Why is it written, It was evening and it was morning the sixth day, with an extra letter hey before Shishi? This teaches that Hashem made a condition with the creations in the world and said to them that if Bnei Yisrael accepts the Torah then you will remain, but if not you will return to Tohu Vavohu, desolation."*

(The extra *hey* that emphasizes a special day six is a reference to the sixth of *Sivan*. This was the day the world was waiting to see if *Bnei Yisrael* would accept the Torah.)

Without Torah the world regresses back to its original state of *Tohu Vavohu*, desolate confusion, as it was in the beginning.

In life we all have our difficult days during which time we search for clarity. We must realize that the Torah has within it the *Ohr* that can brighten every situation.

Bereishis and these opening *pasukim* always follow the season of *Yomim Tovim* that culminated with *Shemini Atzeres*. *Rashi*[9] teaches us that *Shemini Atzeres* is a *Yom Tov* that is not really part of *Succos*. After so many beautiful days of closeness that *Bnei Yisrael* has to Hashem with the celebration of *Rosh Hashana, Yom Kippur* and *Succos,* our time together is coming to a close. *Hashem* beseeches us to please stay one more day and let us be together – the separation anxiety is simply too great. This day that we stay with *Hashem* is the celebration of *Shemini Atzeres*.

Imagine the following scenario. Parents have a son who decides to move to another country. As the family is not blessed with wealth, these parents can only see their child when he visits home once a year for a week. At the end of the week the parents are in such pain and have such sadness that they

---

9. *Parshas Emor, perek* 23, *pasuk* 36

convince the child to stay an extra day. Doesn't that extra day just prolong the inevitable? At the end of that day, won't the family be in the same emotional state of sadness when saying goodbye?

How does *Shemini Atzeres* help in our separation with *Hashem*?

I believe the answer is that on *Shemini Atzeres* we reconnect to the *Ohr Haganuz* that we can hold onto all year long. For a month we build a relationship with *Hashem* with a *shofar*, a *succah*, fasting, waving four *minim* and klopping *al cheit*. Those *mitzvos* and *Yomim Tovim* have concluded. On *Shemini Atzeres* we celebrate *Simchas Torah* as well. We say to *Hashem,* we are with You always as we have the light of the Torah which we will continue to learn and follow. This is our ultimate and constant connection to *Hashem,* which is not bound by a specific time of year or place.

Ki Ner Mitzvah Vetorah Ohr.[10] Torah is the light of our lives, giving us constant clarity!

*

The following story is a true testament to Torah giving complete clarity in this world of darkness.

A few days after Purim in 2005 we were blessed with a beautiful baby girl who has brightened our house, Eliora Malka. The morning after Eliora was born at about 6 am, I received a phone call from my wife and all I hear are tears flowing on the other line. Apparently the nurses *baruch Hashem* noticed that our precious baby was yellow and thereby diagnosed with a terrible disease that was destroying all of her red blood cells. She needed to have a full blood exchange transfusion at only

---

10. *Mishlei, perek* 6, *pasuk* 23.

one day old. *Baruch Hashem* with the help of *Teffilos* she was *zoche* to a complete *Refuah* with no lasting effects.

Along with Eliora's recovery came the news that the blood incompatibility found in our daughter's body would be passed to any of our future children. We were told that the disease was likely to become more intense with each subsequent pregnancy, requiring my *Eishes Chayil* to undergo increasing numbers of blood transfusions until the birth. With the advice of *Gedolim* and doctors, we decided we could handle what *Hashem* would send us, and my wife was *zoche* to become pregnant around September of 2008. We knew it would be a long road and had top high risk pregnancy physicians at our side.

When my wife went in for her first sonogram at 6 weeks, she received heartbreaking news. The baby was lacking a heartbeat and was found to have a deformed head. This was in no way connected to the blood disease we knew would follow. The Doctor felt that the baby was not alive and we should abort, but said if we wanted to, we could wait one week as perhaps there is a minute percentage that the sonogram was mistaken. This devastating news was given on a Tuesday morning.

When delivering this news to our regular OB-GYN, his advice was to abort the next day and move on. "Why prolong the inevitable?" he reasoned. "It will be easier to get this over with and start the healing process." I deeply felt that we should to wait the week suggested us by the first doctor and have the opportunity for *Teffilla* and *Brachos* from *Gedolim*. That is what we decided to do.

Over the next week every *Teffila* was full of deep *Bakashos* for a *Yeshua* and *Refuah*. On Sunday night of that week to-gether with my close friend Binyomin Scharf, I travelled to Brooklyn to seek the *Brachos* of *Gedolim*. Our first stop was the Heilige Skulena Rebba, Rav Yisrael Avraham Portugal, who is very close to my wife's uncle. In Yiddish, the Rebbe gave an intense *Bracha* saying the baby should have "A *Leibedike* heart." After leaving the Rebbe in Boro Park, we headed to the Skverre Rebbe, Rav Dovid Twersky, who was in Flatbush for the week. The Skverre Rebbe was extremely sensitive to the issue and gave a very warm *Bracha* and words of *Chizuk*. I then proceeded to ask the Rebbe if there was a *Kabbalah* or special *Teffillah* I could take upon myself to bring a *Yeshuah*. The Rebbe looked at me and said that there is nothing I needed to do as everything is already okay. I then explained again that there were still two days left to the week deadline and asked again if there was something we should undertake during these two remaining days. The Rebbe again assured me that he understood, and said again that everything is already good.

That Tuesday when my wife went to her doctor for a sonogram we received the miraculous news. The baby had a perfect heartbeat and perfect formation of the head. The doctor had no words to explain what had occurred outside of a miracle. After five blood transfusions during the pregnancy and one after the baby was born, we were *Zocheh* to a beautiful, healthy baby girl. We named her Nesya as she is truly a miracle from *Hashem*!!

The Skvere Rebbe is living a life brightened by the *Ohr Haganuz*. He is able to see and understand the world and all that occurs with clarity we all should yearn for. What may be hidden from our eyes is seen with clarity by the spiritual eyes of our *Tzadikim*!!

Parshas Noach

Never Say "I Can't"

כל־רמש אשר הוא־חי לכם יהיה לאכלה כירק עשב נתתי לכם את־כל־[1]
Every moving living entity is now yours to eat as was the vegetation. I have given you all.

ONE CAN'T IMAGINE the emotions and feelings of Noach after emerging from the *teiva* and viewing a world completely desolate, after being submerged under water for an entire year. I will never forget the morning after Hurricane Sandy driving around the Five Towns and Far Rockaway observing the devastation of that infamous night – seeing lakes of water taking over highways, and cars sitting on front lawns. It was clear that the families who suffered would have to endure a long lasting disaster. Noach found a world completely wiped out. He faced a new reality, a world that would need to be rebuilt from his own family.

Hashem then comes to Noach to bless him and gives him *chizuk* to continue and inhabit the world. The Master of the Universe basically tells Noach, I believe in you and trust in you to not give up. You have the strength to rebuild this barren

---

1. *Parshas Noach, perek* 9, *pasuk* 3.

and shattered world. He then shares with Noach a new way of living. Until this time in history, mankind was only permitted to eat vegetation.[2] Adam, Chava and all of humanity until the *Dor Hamabul* were able to enjoy delicious fruits, vegetables and grains, but were not permitted to enjoy a juicy steak or succulent piece of chicken. No form of living creature was allowed to be eaten. After the *Mabul,* however, Noach is now told that rules have changed. From this point on, he may enjoy living animals as well.

What caused *Hashem* to switch this prohibition to become permitted? And why was this change so crucial to share with Noach immediately after leaving the *teivah*? At a time when Noach must have been so vulnerable and emotional, was it really the best of times to explain his new diet?

Many commentaries have grappled with the reason for this change in the law. I would like to suggest an approach that has given me personal *chizuk* throughout my life. In order to enjoy a delicious piece of rib eye steak, there are many preliminary steps that must be performed. The animal must first be caught and then slaughtered, then skinned and butchered and finally cooked. These acts of preparation can be full of zealousness and apathy. One can even argue that one would be involved in cruelty and savagery.

The *Sefer Hachinuch* famously explains that our actions define who we are.[3] When a person acts in a particular way, his behavior has an impact on his mindset and worldview. A person can't act in a treacherous way and not on some level be influenced in his or her way of thinking.

The *Ribbono Shel Olam* did not want mankind partaking in

2. *Rashi,* ibid.
3. First explained in *Mitzvah* 16.

the ingestion of living animals because of all the preparatory actions that would be needed to preceed their consumption. *Hashem* appreciated the negative affect the handling of the animal could have on a person, leaving him apathetic and cruel towards his fellow. The world was founded on the ideal of *chessed*, and these behaviors would lead man in the completely opposite direction. As the saying goes, "we are what we eat."

The *Dor Hamabul* came along and proved that the world was not progressing along the desired path. Mankind was full of apathy and brutality. Ethics and morality were nonexistent as men treated each other in the worst of ways. Stealing and illicit relations was the norm and decency was absent. The world needed to be destroyed and Noach, the sole moral compass of the universe, was charged with rebuilding.

Hashem at this point in time decided that the rules needed to change. Humanity needed an outlet to somehow express the innate zeal found within us in a positive way. We needed to learn to channel our innate tendencies in a productive way rather than suppress and reject them altogether. Clearly it was the suppression of human nature which had led to these tendencies being expressed in the worst of ways.

As the *Gemara* in *Shabbos*[4] explains, "an individual born under the *mazal*[5] of Mars will surely spill blood." *Rav Ashi* then clarifies that it is up to you whether you become a bandit or channel your abilities towards good and become a *mohel* or *shochet*. Man must not reject a particular character trait, but instead harness it for productive and positive uses.

Therefore, *Hashem*, for the first time allowed man to eat meat, thereby permitting all of the preliminary actions as

4. *Shabbos* 156a.
5. A spiritual force that guides a person.

well. This was done with the vision of providing man with the potential to redirect his natural tendencies of zeal and apathy towards animals, and never channel these traits towards other men. Instead of treating each other poorly, we can now project our natural emotions on the cow we will consume for dinner.

Perhaps this is also the understanding of another very difficult *Parsha* in the Torah. In the beginning of *Parshas Ki Teitzei*[6] we learn of the *Isha Yefas Toar*. Under certain circumstances, after several particular steps are taken, a Jewish soldier is permitted to marry a captured woman during wartime. At first glance, this entire *parsha* is difficult to comprehend as it would seem that an act that should be greatly dissuaded by the Torah is being allowed. Temptation and illicit relations are of the gravest of sins in the Torah. Again, *Hashem* is telling us that he understands the needs of His holy children and occasionally will adapt the system to make it achievable and attainable.

While we now understand why *Hashem* permitted Noach and his family to eat meat, we must still ask why this command needed to be told to Noach just moments after leaving the *teivah*.

Upon leaving the ark, Noach was seemingly not only overwhelmed by needing to rebuild the world from scratch, but was also doubtful as to how the new generation that would arise would reverse course from the previous and behave in a more dignified way? After living with a generation of wicked individuals which he was unable to influence over many years and attempts, his hope for the next generation of mankind was dimmed. *Hashem* therefore is now teaching and instilling within Noach the insight needed to prevent history from repeating itself. The world would not continue to abide by the

---

6. *Perek* 21, *pasukim* 10–14.

same laws, but would be changed to ensure success. Noach was to take the inspiration and follow the path paved by *Hashem* to be a partner in the reconstruction of the world.

With this understanding of why *Hashem* changed the law of eating meat at that time, we can gain much encouragement in our *Avodas Hashem*. There are times when one might feel that a particular area of *Avodah* is just too difficult. It is just too hard to set aside serious time to study Torah with all the responsibilities and obligations of my day. Am I really expected to daven with a minyan three times a day, each and every day? Is it possible for a person to never speak *Lashon Harah*? Can I stay away from the pool when in Miami for Pesach? We learn from this *Parsha* that every area of *Avodas Hashem* is accessible and that we are very capable of keeping and following its demands. The words "I can't" need to be obliterated from our vocabulary when it comes to serving The One Above. By the fact that *Hashem* decided to change the rules in a select few instances, as he did with permitting meat after the *Mabul* and permitting an *eishes yefas toar*, we can infer that any other area of *Avodas Hashem* that has not been changed is on account of the fact that we are very capable of fulfilling the desires of *Hashem*. At times being an *Eved Hashem* is hard, but we must never use the words, "I can't." We can gain confidence that Hashem believes in us and that we can achieve the Torah's vision for us, for if this were not the case, the rules would have been changed to make it so.

*

Over the years I have learned and been influenced by many special Tzaddikim that I have the *zchus* to refer to as Rebbi. The Rosh Yeshiva of the Mir, Harav Nosson Tzvi Finkel *ztz"l*, was a *Gadol Hador* to the world in Torah and *Tzidkus*, but personally was a foundation of my life as a *Yid*. From the time I began to attend his weekly *Erev Shabbos* shmooze in his house while I was still learning in *Kerem Beyavneh,* I immediately needed to stay close to the Rosh Yeshiva whenever possible. Eventually, I had the *zchus* to learn in the Mir for a *zman* and further strengthen my *kesher.* I was constantly asking advice and learning from the Rosh Yeshiva. It was a relationship that continued after leaving the Yeshiva, as the highlight of every trip I would take to *Eretz Yisrael* was spending time with the Rosh Yeshiva and attending his *Erev Shabbos* shmooze. The final time I was *zoche* to be in the Rosh Yeshiva's presence was exactly one month before his *Pettira* on *Yud Aleph Tishrei* 5772, the day after Yom Kippur, and the parting kiss is still felt. So much of who I am today is owed to the Rosh Yeshiva. Who better to learn from to be an *Amel Betorah* and *Eved Hashem* with *Messiras Nefesh* and *Simcha* than the Rosh Yeshiva *ztz"l*!!

There have already been books written about the Rosh Yeshiva that are inspirational to all who read them. I would like to just add two personal accounts that I encountered with the Rosh Yeshiva. As is well known the Rosh Yeshiva suffered from Parkinson's disease for the last 20 years of his life, including essentially the entire time I knew him. He often had very little control of his body and although never complained, was clearly in pain. He had every reason to say I can't, but never did.

One Shabbos in *Elul,* I had the *Zchus* to eat *Shabbos Seudah* at the home of the Rosh Yeshiva. The meal was very special, having the opportunity to witness the Rosh Yeshiva in his family setting. I will never forget after the first course the Rosh Yeshiva himself with his hands shaking, proceeded to clear away my fish plate. It was a very simple act coming from a very big man. *Midos* and care for others is our first priority. The words "I can't" were just not part of the Rosh Yeshiva's vocabulary – not only in his learning, but in his *Bein Adam Lechaveiro.*

On a similar note, when I was leaving *Eretz Yisrael* after

my second year in Kerem Beyavneh I went to the home of the Rosh Yeshiva to ask advice regarding how to be successful in various areas of *avodas Hashem* when returning back to America. I spent 45 minutes with the Rosh Yeshiva receiving words of wisdom that continue to inspire me until today. During our conversation the Rosh Yeshiva had a stack of 500 pieces of paper in front of him. The papers were thank-you notes to be sent to those patrons of the Yeshiva who attended the Mir dinner. The entire 45 minutes the Rosh Yeshiva was personally signing each one, one by one. Each signature took him between 20–40 seconds, as his shaky hands would often not be as cooperative as he wished. He could easily have had a stamp made with his signature and had someone in the office stamp every note. Yet, the Rosh Yeshiva understood how happy each individual would be after receiving his personal signature. To make someone else feel good had no limits and no task was too difficult!! Never say I can't. As the famous slogan of Nike says so well, "Just Do It."

This custom of the Rosh Yeshiva continued until his final days. When I visited the Rosh Yeshiva a month before his *Petirah* I gave him a small donation for the yeshiva as *Hakaras Hatov*. A week after the Rosh Yeshiva's *Petirah* I received a thank-you letter personally signed by the Rosh Yeshiva. The envelope was marked *Yud Aleph Cheshvon*, the day of the Rosh Yeshiva's *Petirah*!!

Parshas Lech Lecha

Sacrifices of Today Create Miracles of Tomorrow

ואעשך לגוי גדול ואברכך ואגדלה שמך והיה ברכה[1]

I will make you into a great nation and I will bless you. I will make your name great, and you will have the power of blessing others.

WHAT *YID* IS NOT CONSTANTLY SEARCHING for *bracha* in their life? Sometimes it seems that the 11th commandment is Thou Shall Go to *Gedolim* for *Brachos*. We ask *Tzadikim* for *Brachos* in *Parnassa*, for *Nachas* from children, for *shiduchim*, and any and every type of *yeshua*. How amazing must it have been for Avraham to receive these very same *Brachos* from *Hakadosh Baruch Hu, Bechvodo Uveatzmo*.

When analyzing the *Brachos* that Avraham received, one *bracha* stands out as perplexing. To be blessed that he will become a great nation is the *Bracha* introducing the formation of *Bnei Yisrael*. To be blessed that he will be wealthy, as *Rashi*[2] explains the blessing of *Va'avorechacha*, also makes sense. The

---

1. *Parshas Lech Lecha, perek 12, pasuk 2.*
2. *Rashi,* ibid.

only way to serve *Hashem* completely, including giving *tzeda-kah* and helping others, requires money. Yet, the third *Bracha,* of assuring that the name of Avraham would be made great and famous, is puzzling. *Chazal* teach us that *gayvah,* haughtiness, is the worst of all character traits. The *Gemara*[3] goes as far as to compare *gayvah* to *Avodah Zarah.* Why would Avraham be blessed with fame? Was Avraham looking for honor and renown?

Rashi[4] explains that this *Bracha* does not mean as we initially suspected, that the name of Avraham will become famous and respected by humanity, but rather that literally his name will become larger. The name of Avram will be changed from Avram to Avraham.

Why was the letter *Hey* added? What is the significance of this addition?

אלה תולדות השמים והארץ בהבראם ביום עשות יקוק א־להים ארץ
ושמים[5]

These are the offspring of the heavens and earth when they were created on the day that Hashem created earth and heavens.

Rashi[6] explains that the word "*Behibaram*" can be read as *Be-Hey baram. Hashem* created the world with the letter *hey.* The formation of the Hebrew letter *hey* is completely open on the bottom with an additional small opening in the upper left cor-ner. The *hey* being open on the bottom represents our world, full of *tayva* and *gashmius,* which are chasms into which one can easily fall. The small opening at the top represents the way

3. Sotah 4b.
4. *Rashi Lech Lecha,* 12:2.
5. *Parshas Bereishis, perek* 2, *pasuk* 4.
6. Ibid.

back in for those devoted to do *Teshuva* and climb back into *Beis Hashem*.

The *Rabbeinu Bchaya*[7] explains that the root word *teva*, usually defined as the natural order of the world, has an additional meaning of sinking or drowning. The essence of this world is that it brings one to sink to the lowest of places. However, one can transcend the natural forces of this world and live a supernatural life above *teva* and climb back to the highest of spiritual heights.

Avraham grew up in the world of *teva* full of *avodah zarah* and *tayva*. He rose to the challenge to become the first *baal teshuva*, to climb back in through the top of the *hey*. He acted *lamaleh min hatevah*, in a supernatural way, as he passed test after test. He was willing to throw himself into a fire and even sacrifice his 37 year old son for *Hashem*. He was not following the usual laws of the natural world of *teva*, the world that brings one to sink. Through his example, Avraham defined the purpose of man and the purpose of creation. We are all here to rise above nature. Avraham's name is therefore gifted with an extra *hey*. Added to his name is the letter that created the world as he was the quintessential example of who *Hashem* wants in His world. In fact, with the added *hey*, Avraham's name now has the same letters as the word "*Behibaram.*" He has fulfilled the purpose of creation and therefore embodies it. His name with this *hey* also corresponds to the numerical value, or *gematria,* of 248, representing the 248 positive *mitzvos*. These are the 248 opportunities man has to rise above the world and act supernaturally.

We are all children of Avraham and must follow in his footsteps. Often it is difficult in the world we live in, full of

---

7. *Hakdama to Parshas Massei*

responsibilities and pressures, to serve *Hashem* in the way that we know we should. It is not always easy to daven as long as we would like, or learn as much as we once did. We must create miracles above the natural world and each live as Avraham.

ויוצא אתו החוצה ויאמר הבט־נא השמימה וספר הכוכבים אם־תוכל
לספר אתם ויאמר לו כה יהיה זרעך[8]

Hashem took him outside and said, "Look up at heaven and count the stars if you are able." Hashem then said to him, "So too will be your children."

The Midrash[9] explains that *Hashem* took Avraham outside the universe above the entire sky and said, "stare down and count the stars below." Rav Avraham Shorr[10] explains that *Hashem* was teaching Avraham that you have the ability to rise above nature. He then proceeds to add "*Ko Yehye Zarecha*," so too will be your children. Avraham was promised that each and every one of us has the ability to tap into the *koach* of Avraham and rise above the natural limits of this world.

When we are willing to go above and beyond and sacrifice for *Hashem,* we are connecting to this same promise. The promise was made with the word *ko.* The *gematria* of *ko* is 25, which is identical to the 25 letters in the *pasuk* of *Shema Yisrael,* the *pasuk* that is the symbol of being above *teva* and sacrificing for *Hashem.*

When we are willing to sacrifice for *Hashem,* as Avraham did, and live a life of *mesiras nefesh, Hashem* will reciprocate in the form of miracles. This is what we were *zoche* to experience in the Channukah story. Thirteen weak yeshiva *bochurim*

---

8. *Parshas Lech Lecha, perek* 15, *pasuk* 5.
9. *Bereishis Rabba,* 44:12.
10. *Halekach Vehalibuv, Channukah, p.* 96.

went above nature and were willing to sacrifice their lives for *Hashem*. In response, *Hashem* delivered the miracle of Channukah. The *Sfas Emes*[11] says that each of the 10 tests of Avraham brought a miracle into the world. This is also why that same word *ko,* used to instill this *middah* within each of us, if spelled out *bemillui*[12] is in *gematria* 110. The *gematria* of *neis*, a miracle, is also exactly 110.

When we are willing to sacrifice for *Hashem* and live a life like Avraham of *lemalah min hatevah*, we will be *zoche* to miracles from above for all of *Bnei Yisrael.*

*

The following story is just one example of this relationship with *Hashem*.

For my High School years I studied in The Marsha Stern Talmudical Academy otherwise known as MTA. One of my classmates was Chaim[13] who was the type of student who made any Rebbi who walked into the room immediately want to walk back out. Chaim struggled with *Yiddishkeit* in every way one can imagine. It was early on in 11th grade that Chaim was finally asked to leave the Yeshiva. Being that I was not really close to him, we did not stay in touch from that point on.

Towards the end of 11th grade, I was walking in the hallway outside the Yeshiva University *Beis Medrash* that was located on the first floor of MTA. I suddenly noticed laying on top of a pile of *Shaimos* a pair of *Teffillin* that looked familiar. Although there was no name embroidered on the bag, I knew they were Chaim's *Teffillin*, as I used to daven next to him every morning.

---

11. *Sfas Emes, Parshas Vayeira, year* 5635.
12. The *millui* of a word is to fill in the missing letters from a word when sounding out each letter separately. In our example of the word *ko* the millui would be *kuf pey hey hey.*
13. Name has been changed.

I took them home and hoped to find Chaim and return them to him soon. Unfortunately I never ended up getting in touch with Chaim and as time passed, I eventually totally forgot about the Teffillin which waited longingly in the closet of my parent's house.

During my third year out of High School I was registered in Yeshiva University for the fall semester. That year Elul began in the middle of August and I therefore had the amazing *zchus* to learn for Elul *zman* in Yeshivas Mir Yerushalayim. For the small price of missing a few classes in college, I was *zoche* to learn *Makkos* with *Rashi* and *Tosfos* and build a life changing relationship with the Rosh Yeshiva Harav Nosson Tzvi Finkel *ztz"l*.

A few days before Yom Kippur I was walking in the streets of Beis Yisrael when I saw a young man from a distance who looked very familiar. As he moved closer I realized it was Chaim, but a very different looking Chaim. In place of a T-shirt, jeans and a baseball cap were white shirt, dark pants and a large velvet Yarmulka. We embraced and immediately started to catch up as all *Yidden* would. I found out that after leaving high school, Chaim went to learn in a Yeshiva for boys who need a lot of *chizuk* and was *Baruch Hashem* very successful. He was now learning in Yeshivas Toras Moshe for 12 hours a day.

At that moment, Hashem reminded me about the *Teffillin* that have been hidden away in the closet of my parent's house for the past 4 years. Although I was embarrassed that I never returned them until now, I was so excited to tell Chaim that I had kept them for him. After sharing my news and watching the excited reaction of my old friend's face, Chaim shared with me where he was headed when *Hashem* brought us together at that moment. Of course after losing his *Teffillin,* Chaim had gotten a new pair, but about 2 weeks prior to our meeting he lost those as well. For 2 weeks he was searching high and low and finally gave up. *When Hashem brought us back together after 4 years, Chaim was on the way to purchase a new pair of* Teffillin.

I was able to have my father send the *Teffillin* with someone coming to Eretz Yisrael for Succos, and finally return them to their holy owner in the most opportune of times.

Chaim decided to sacrifice all that he was connected to and start living a life above *teva* for the *Ribbono Shel Olam*. As seen in this story, *Hashem* responds to such dedication *lemaaleh min hatevah*.

Parshas Vayera

To Make the Will of Hashem Our Will

ויהי אחר הדברים האלה והא־להים נסה את־אברהם ויאמר אליו
אברהם ויאמר הנני: ויאמר קח־נא את־בנך את־יחידך אשר־אהבת
את־יצחק ולך־לך אל־ארץ המריה והעלהו שם לעלה על אחד ההרים
אשר אמר אליך[1]

*And it was after these words that Hashem tested Avraham.
Hashem called Avraham by name and Avraham answered,
"I am here." Hashem said to take his only son, the one that
he loves, Yitzchak, and go to the land of Moriah. There bring
Yitzchak up on a mountain that I will tell you to be a burnt
offering.*

EVERY *PARSHA* IN THE TORAH is extremely meaningful and
full of foundational life teachings. As the Lubavitcher Rebbe
used to say, "A *Yid* must live with the *parsha*." *Parshas Vayera,*
being my bar mitzvah *sedrah,* has a special place in my heart.
Moreover there is no story in all of *Chumash* that I have gained
more inspiration from than *Akeidas Yitzchak.* It is not by chance
that one is supposed to recite this story every day in our *Teffilos,*
and is additionally a focal point throughout the *Yamim Noraim.*

---

1. *Parshas Vayaera,* 22:1–2.

When analyzing the story of *Akeidas Yitzchak* one can not imagine how it was possible for Avraham Avinu to be willing to kill his son. Yitzchak was already a 37 year old man and even more strikingly, he was also the man through which the future of *Bnei Yisrael* was previously guaranteed to Avraham by *Hashem*. And yet, Avraham was now being asked to contradict his entire life teachings and future posterity, and sacrifice Yitzchak?

On the flip side, one can ask, was it really possible for Avraham to fail? Avraham was asked by *Hashem* himself via a prophecy to carry out this difficult task. Could Avraham have said no to *Hashem*? The reason each of us struggles at times to serve *Hashem* in the way He wants is because we are not receiving prophetic commandments from *Hashem* Himself. I would like to believe if I was asked by *Hashem* to do anything, I would surely listen.

My Rebbe, Harav Mendel Blachman, suggested the following explanation regarding how impressive the test of *Akeidas Yitzchak* truly was. The Rambam[2] explains that when any *navi* was to receive a prophecy the *Navi* would first fall into a spiritual comatose slumber. The *navi* would then obtain a *navuah* hidden within a dream. The dream would be similar to our dreams with no clear message from above. The *navi* would need to utilize their *chochmah* to interpet the dream and understand the prophesy being given. Only *Moshe Rabbeinu* would prophesize via an *aspaklaria meirah* and receive a clear message from above. Avraham was a *Navi* like all other *Neveim* and therefore needed to interpet the vision of a potentially confusing dream.

When Avraham was given the revelation leading to *Akeidas Yitzchak,* it was not as it seems in the *pasukim*. Avraham was never asked in a straight forward way to kill Yitzchak. Avraham

---

2. *Rambam, Hilchos Yesodei Hatorah, perek 7.*

could have interpreted his dream with his own subjective desires guiding his understanding. After receiving such a dream it would be easy to say there is no way *Hashem* wants me to kill my son, the one who he promised would be the future of *Bnei Yisrael*. It must be that I am only being asked to symbolically offer my son to *Hashem* by binding him atop *Har Moriah*.

The test of *Akeidas Yitzchak* was for Avraham to ignore all of his desires and thoughts and objectively be one with the desires of *Hashem*. Avraham was able to say that although I don't want to do this and have the power to infuse my own thoughts into this situation, I will be as intellectually honest as possible and only serve the One Above. I will see this prophesy thru the lenses of *Hashem*.

This is the ultimate test of Avraham and the ultimate test of mankind. How often do we rationalize our actions and convince ourselves we are acting within the confines of *Hashem's* desires, when it is in fact directly against the Will of *Hashem*? The true *eved Hashem* is just that, a servant of *Hashem*. We are not in this world to rationalize our desires and temptations as if they are the will of *Hashem*, but rather to make the will of *Hashem* our will. As the *Mishna* in *Avos*[3] says we must make our wants the wants of *Hashem*.

I believe this idea can help answer another complexity in the story of the *Akeida*.

> ויאמר אל־תשלח ידך אל־הנער ואל־תעש לו מאומה כי עתה ידעתי
> כי־ירא א־להים אתה ולא חשכת את־בנך את־יחידך ממני[4]
> *And he [the angel] said, "Don't stretch out your hand to the boy or do anything to him because now I know that you are a God fearing man and you did not withhold your only son from me."*

---

3. *Avos, perek 2, mishna 4.*
4. *Parshas Vayaera, perek 22, pasuk 12.*

Why does the Torah tell us that only now Avraham is considered a *Baal Yiras Shamayim*? How could it be that until *Akeidas Yitzchak* it was not crystal clear that Avraham was in awe of *Hashem*? Didn't Avraham previously allow himself to be thrown into a fiery furnace instead of serving idols? Isn't this the same Avraham that left his homeland and family to journey to an unkown land? What does it take to be considered someone who possesses *Yiras Shamayim*? Is it possible for any of us to reach a level of *Yiras Shamayim*? The Ohr Hachaim[5] explains in *Parshas Eikev* that the only thing that *Hashem* asks of us is to be a *Yirei Shamayim*. I therefore deeply hope it would be attainable for all of *Bnei Yisrael* to achieve.

Every test until *Akeidas Yitzchak* was carried out by Avraham with an understanding of why it had to be fulfilled. There was an appreciation of the reason behind the will of *Hashem*. This gave Avraham the strength to succeed. Although nobody would want to jump into a fire, Avraham, who believed in *Hashem* and was spreading monotheism throughout the world, would not serve *Avodah Zarah* under any circumstance. To leave one's homeland is difficult, but being told he would become a great nation and have only blessing is very compelling. *Akeidas Yitzchak* demanded that Avraham act in a way contrary to all of his previously espoused beliefs and his deepest desires. It is well known that one form of *avodah zarah* during Avraham's time that he would preach against involved parents sacrificing their children to their gods. By following through with the *akeida,* Avraham would be viewed as a colossal hypocrite to the outside world and would be forced to live for the remainder of his life with the knowledge that he killed his son. There is no question that the killing of Yitzchak would be carried out

---

5. *Parshas Eikev, perek* 10, *pasuk* 12.

against all of his desires with no comprehension. This would define Avraham as someone who possesses true *yiras Hashem*, awe of *Hashem*. Only when one's actions are contrary to one's own understanding and desires can someone truly be crowned with the title *Yiras Shamyaim*. To be able to interpet his prophecy objectively and be willing to sacrifice his own son makes Avraham the model of *yiras shamayim*.

Although *Bezras Hashem* we believe the *nisayon* of *Akeidas Yitzchak* will never fall upon any member of *Bnei Yisrael* again, we are all constantly tested in the same vein. Are we true *Yirei Shamayim*? Are we willing to place the will of *Hashem* above our own, or do we rationalize our actions and reinterpet the desires of *Hashem*?

*

The following story on its surface is one portraying the greatnes of a *tzaddik*, but behind the scenes is the portrayal of an example of *Akeidas Yitzchak*:

We could argue whether it is the *koach* of *Teffillah* or some form of *ruach hakodesh* that allows our *Tzaddikim* to have abilities above nature, but that it is a fact is indisputable. One such *Tzaddik* in our days is the *mekubal* and grandson of the Baba Sali, Rebbe Dovid Abuchatzeira. I have been *zoche* to meet with Rebbe Dovid many times and each time I have walked away with both tremendous inspiration as well as a sense of calm in life. Here is what occurred on one of those special meetings.

A few years ago, I walked into Rebbe Dovid and as usual he immediately gave me the feeling that he was my best friend in the world. I proceeded to ask him for a *Bracha* for a special *Talmid* of mine. This young man was at the time dating a girl for a very long time wanting to marry her. The problem was, based on the *Psak* of Maran Harav Elyashiv, it was prohibited for him to marry her. Many people close to this young man were trying hard to break off this relationship, but to no avail. In fact the week before, the boy's Rebbi from Eretz Yisrael who was visiting the States told me that after meeting with his *Talmid* he finally realized there is no more hope. After explaining the details to Rebbe Dovid he used the boys name as *roshei teivos* for *pasukim* as *brachos* and then added his own *brachos*. Rebbe Dovid then looked at me and smiled and said very soon everything will be fine. After a year of *Teffilos* and *brachos* from many *Gedolim* it was hard to be completely comforted, but I exited Yeshivas Abir Yaakov into the streets of Nahariya that day with renewed hope.

That meeting took place on a Thursday afternoon in January. The very next Thursday when I was back in America I received a phone call from the young man's father. With great joy he told me that we need to share in a *Seudas Hodaah*. His son seemingly out of nowhere had ended the relationship.

Of course one could say that this outcome was purely based on the *bracha* of the *tzaddik*, but I would argue that while there is no question that Rebbe Dovid played a major role in the *yeshuah*, ultimately the young man had to perform his *Akeidah*. His deep desires and wants were strongly in favor of spending the rest of his life by the side of this woman that he loved. Yet, this *Talmid* was able to dig deep within and tap into the *Yiras Shamayim* ingrained within all of us from Avraham *Avinu* and act according to the will of *Hashem*. Today this young man is happily married to a wonderful young woman.

He passed his *Akeidas Yitzchak*. Are we passing ours?

Parshas Chayei Sarah

A Marriage of *Chessed*

ויקם שדה עפרון אשר במכפלה אשר לפני ממרא השדה והמערה
אשר־בו וכל־העץ אשר בשדה אשר בכל־גבלו סביב: לאברהם למקנה
לעיני בני־חת בכל באי שער־עירו:[1] כי אל־ארצי ואל־מולדתי תלך
ולקחת אשה לבני ליצחק[2]

The field of Efron that was in Machpeila facing Mamreh together with the cave and all the trees in the field within its border was sold to Avraham in front of Bnei Cheis and all those at the gate of the city. Go to my land and birthplace to take a wife for my son Yitzchak.

ARGUABLY THE MOST IMPORTANT commitment that a person will make in life is the choice of a spouse. Together you will share your aspirations and dreams and build the future of *Bnei Yisrael*. How does the Torah guide us in reaching this life-long decision? What is the Torah's list of priorities one should make sure to check off when choosing a spouse?

The opening *Gemara* in *Meseches Kiddushin*[3] teaches about

---

1. *Parshas Chayei Sarah, perek 23, pasukim 17–18.*
2. Perek 24, pasuk 4.
3. *Kiddushin 2a.*

the basis for using a ring as a means towards halachik engagement at our weddings. This first part of the marriage process can be fulfilled when a man gives a woman money or an object with monetary value. This exchange, when performed in front of two witnesses, together with a statement of desired engagement, will deem the couple halachically engaged. Yes, that expensive diamond engagement ring given months earlier, has little halachik significance. This *halacha* is learned from a comparison of similar words used by both the *pasuk* teaching about marriage and the *pasuk* describing Avraham's purchase of the *Maaras Hamachpeila*. In both cases the word *Kach*, to take, is used and accordingly, *chazal* learn from one to the other based on the principal of *gazeiras shavah*. Since Avraham purchased the *Maaras Hamachpeila* with money, so too we are able to become engaged with money or a ring with monetary value.

Although *Chazal's* usage of *gazeiras shavah* needs no assistance, we can ask if there are any deeper connections between the purchase of a burial plot for Sarah and the first step in marriage? Doesn't it seem a little counterintuitive to learn from the death of Avraham's wife how to enter into that type of union? Of course, when analyzing our *Parsha*, it is interesting to note that juxtaposed immediately following the burial of Sarah is the story of finding a wife for Yitzchak. This does shed some light on the comparison made in *Torah Shebaal Peh* based on the connection in *Torah Shebiksav*. What, therefore, is the fundamental lesson in marriage to be discovered from this comparison?

The Torah in our *parsha* uses 67 *pasukim* to discuss what led to the marriage between Yitzchak and Rivkah. Knowing how we often learn a halacha from one extra letter, undoubtedly this story needs to be studied well. When looking over this *perek* one will only find one prerequisite that was needed as Eliezer searched for a spouse for his master's son. There is only one item on Rivkah's Shidduch resume that needed to be checked off. Yitzchak's future wife needed to be a giving, empathetic individual full of concern for others. She needed to show care to Eliezer and his camels by offering not only him to drink, but also his flock. Being the daughter and sister of cheating idol worshippers is no deterrent, as long as she is a *Baalas Chessed*.

ויבאה יצחק האהלה שרה אמו ויקח את־רבקה ותהי־לו לאשה
ויאהבה וינחם יצחק אחרי אמו[4]

Yitzchak took Rivkah into the tent of his mother Sarah and took her for a wife. He loved her and was comforted concerning the loss of his mother.

When Eliezer brings Rivkah to Yitzchak he is finally consoled following the loss of his mother. *Rashi*[5] points out that Rivkah literally was able to fill the void of Sarah's loss by restoring the three miracles that occurred in Sarah's tent: A candle would be lit from one erev Shabbos to the next, the dough was full of blessing, and a cloud of honor would hover over the tent. The restoring of these three miracles with Rivkah's arrival was surely a validation that Eliezer chose correctly.

When analyzing the Midrash[6] quoted by *Rashi* concerning these three miracles one finds a fourth miracle omitted by *Rashi*. The tent of Sarah was always open to the poor. Why would *Rashi* leave out a practice that was surely continued by Rivkah?

We can suggest that being a *Baalas Chessed* was the entrance exam needed to be considered as a bride for Yitzchak. It was

---

4. *Chayei Sarah, perek* 24, *pasuk* 67.
5. *Ibid.*
6. *Bereishis Rabba* 60:16.

surely no *chidush* to Yitzchak that Eliezer would bring such a young woman home. No marriage should be considered if there isn't belief that one's future spouse is a *Baal Chessed*. There is therefore no need to emphasize such a detail.

The Torah is surely teaching us not only who to look for in a wife, but also a fundamental principle for maintaining a healthy and blossoming marriage. Marriage is the beginning of one's independent life. The world we live in is full of responsibility and needs that can easily pull a person far from a focus on the One Above. One needs to earn a living, pay bills, change diapers and clean the house among numerous other seemingly mundane activities that can consume much of one's married life. Having to spend so much time attending to one's physical needs can cause one to forget the world of spirituality. In marriage, as in the life of a bachelor, our relationship with *Hashem* and *ruchnius* must continue to play center stage. Yet this becomes much more difficult as one realizes that gone are the days when he can learn Torah and *daven* exclusively without other responsibilities.

A *Baal Chesed*, someone who is always looking to give and help others, uplifts every activity that occupies his/her time into an act of spirituality. One can transform all that one is involved in into acts of *chessed* and ways to connect to *Hashem*. *Hashem* is the ultimate *Baal Chessed* specifically in His connection to our world. The entire creation of the world and the constant bond to everything in this universe is solely based on the *Chessed of Hashem*. When giving to others one is emulating *Hashem* and thereby developing a deeper relationship with Hashem. Everything we do can be elevated to an act of *chessed* if the needs of others are in our mind. This is especially true if we are proactive *Baalei Chessed* and not merely reactive *Baalei Rachamim*. It is one thing to help others when seeing them in tears. It is a whole other level to always be searching to help others and to elevate all that you do to a level of *chessed*.

With *chessed* one can change every act of life to a meaningful and spiritual one. Whether it is earning money in the office, or cleaning the house, if one has the needs of others in mind, one is involved in an act of *Hashem*!!

Eliezer understood this value not only from his years as a servant to Avraham, the *ish chessed*, but from the commandment of Avraham to him concerning who to find as a wife for Yitzchak.

> ואשביעך ביקוק א־להי השמים וא־להי הארץ אשר לא־תקח אשה
> לבני מבנות הכנעני אשר אנכי יושב בקרבו[7]
>
> *I will make you swear by the God of heavens and earth that you don't take a wife for my son from the daughters of Canaan among whom I dwell in their midst.*

Why didn't Avraham desire a daughter-in-law from *Canaan*? It is not like Besual and Lavan are the best of people. Additionally what is added and emphasized by the end of the *pasuk*, "among whom I dwell in their midst"? What was Avraham's message in these seemingly unnecessary words?

> אנכי עמד בין־יקוק וביניכם בעת ההוא להגיד לכם את־דבר יקוק כי
> יראתם מפני האש ולא־עליתם בהר לאמר[8]
>
> *I was standing between you and Hashem at that time to tell you the word of Hashem because you were afraid to ascend the mountain due to the fire.*

One can understand this *pasuk* as teaching us that focusing only on oneself starkly contrasts with a relationship with

---

7. *Chayei Sarah, perek 24, pasuk 3.*
8. *Parshas Vaeschanan, perek 5, pasuk 5.*

Hashem. Anochi, being concerned with the "I," is the strongest barrier between *Hashem* and any person. This is the deeper message behind the opening words of the pasuk which states "I was standing between you and *Hashem*". There is no place to be self centered in Judaism. Obviously this state is the complete opposite of *a Baal Chessed*.

Avraham was telling Eliezer that these are the ways of Canaan, so please stay away from them for my son. The people of Canaan were only concerned with themselves, apathetic to the needs of others. This is what was meant in Avraham stating concerning Canaan that "I dwell in their midst". Avraham was not stating the obvious, that he lived there, but rather that the people of Canaan were only concerned with "I". I need a *Baal Chessed* for Yitzchak and everything else will work itself out.

Now we can understand the comparison between the purchase of *Maaras Hamachpeila* and *Kiddushin*. The acquisition of the burial plot for Sarah was in order to honor Sarah after her death. It is well know that toiling over the respect for the dead is known as *Chessed Shel Emes*. This form of kindness is the most authentic and meaningful act one can perform, as it is clear that the kindness is being done not for future expected respect or retribution, as the one benefiting has no ability to repay or even acknowledge the favor. The Torah is teaching each of us that this same level of *Chessed* should also be practiced in the daily functions of a marriage. We must always be in a state of giving, with no mindset of gaining in return. We can thereby raise up our daily life with *Chessed Shel Emes* as our driving force.

There is no question that all of *Shalom Bayis* is dependent on this principle. *Bezras Hashem* we will discuss that concept of giving in a marriage in *Parshas Mikeitz*. We must realize it is not merely the glue that strengthens our relationship with our wife, but is the foundation of ensuring that the long stage of life called marriage is lived full of *ruchnius* and meaning.

*

The following is a true story of *Chessed Shel Emes*:

During the summer of 2013 I was *zoche* to be *Mesadder Kiddushin* at the *Chassuna* of a close *talmid*, Mordechai Katz who was marrying Tamar Weinstein. The Chassuna was taking place on a Thursday night in the Roemer Shul in Teaneck, N.J. The *Chassuna* was called for 6:00 pm with *Chuppah* at 7:00, which we all know really means 7:30 pm. Being *Messader Kiddushin,* I wanted to be on time and therefore left my house at 4:45 with plenty of time to spare. My *talmid* Tuvia Aharon Barth joined me for the ride and after checking Waze for the best route, we were on our way.

The first leg of our trip was uneventful as we were actually making excellent time. We arrived at the Cross Bronx Expressway, more than half way into our trip, in about half an hour. The Cross Bronx however was a virtual parking lot. I don't mean cars were moving slowly, rather they were all in a complete standstill. Listening to the radio we found out that the George Washington Bridge that we would need to cross in order to enter New Jersey was completely closed as there was a Caravan on fire on the lower level. Every highway leading to the bridge was in lockdown.

I immediately started maneuvering around the cars to pull onto the shoulder so I could drive toward the first exit. I exited the highway into the Bronx and with the help of my father who is a human GPS, was able to travel via the streets through the Bronx to arrive at the bridge. This was a lengthy journey, but with my PBA Rabbi card ready to be used and a wedding that I needed to make sure would happen, I may have treated a few red lights as Stop signs. As an added wrinkle, the *Kesuvah* and

Tenaim were in the car with me as the couple felt I would be most responsible, which would make it even more difficult for anyone else to fill in as *Messader Kiddushin* if I didn't make it.

As we inched closer to the bridge, the traffic began to pick up and we started to move very slowly. The upper level of the bridge did open by this time, but it seemed as though all of New York was headed toward it. I slowly made my way and finally arrive at the entrance to the bridge. It was already close to 7 and I estimated it would take another 45 minutes considering the traffic. After committing to cross over the bridge on the upper level that was jam packed, suddenly the lower level reopens and of course the first cars are flying across. I decide that although there is a foot and a half high and 3 foot wide cement barrier in between my car and the lower level, I need to go for it and get to this *Chassunah*. I turn my wheel right and slam on the gas pedal. The car climbs up the barrier and then suddenly comes crashing down on top of it. Here I was at 7 pm with my car dangling on top of a cement barrier dividing the upper and lower levels of the GW Bridge. Many thoughts immediately entered my head: (1) My wife is going to kill me. (2) I just destroyed our car. (3) The *Chassuna*!!

I tell Tuvya Aharon to try to get out to push. He tries to no avail as trying to push a car with its wheels dangling is similar to trying to move a house. I personally came to this realization when I got out and tried to help.

So here we are standing outside in our suits staring at our car as other cars pass by gazing in amazement with some choice words as well.

Suddenly I make eye contact with a bearded *Yid* in a beard with a striped shirt driving a black Range Rover about thirty feet from where I was standing. He was passing on the side I came from to travel over the upper level. I understand from hand motion with no words exchanged that he wants to use his car as a battering ram to push my car over the barrier. I told Tuvia Aharon to get in, and although he thought I was crazy, he jumps in the car. Within a moment we feel a strong push and my car flies over the barrier into the lane of the lower level and *Baruch Hashem* I press on the gas and the car actually works. As I turn back to thank my hero I can only wave as he is already off to his destination. We arrive at the *Chassuna* about 10 minutes later, in time for everything to run smoothly and beautifully.

This was the Thursday after *Parshas Pinchas* and we all know *Chazal* teach us that Pinchas is Eliyahu. I deeply believe that this *Tzaddik* was Eliyahu himself. One of my Talmidim asked me, "Isn't Eliyahu supposed to be riding on a donkey?" First of all surely Eliyahu's means of transportation would change with the times, and yesterday's donkey is today's Range Rover. Secondly Chamor, a donkey, in *Gematria* is 254 and Range in *Gematria* with the *kollel*[9] is also 254!!

In the small chance that this was not Eliyahu, we can say "*Mi Kaamcha Yisrael.*" What a *tzaddik* who was willing to take his own expensive car and I am sure scratch it up, and perhaps create a dent to help a *Yid* in need. He of course had no clue that I was *Messader Kiddushin* with all the documents in the car and his act of *chessed* saved a *chassuna*. At that moment, a Range Rover on the GW Bridge was elevated into a means towards performing an act of *Chessed Shel Emes*. We must always be searching to elevate all that we do to connect to *Hashem*.

---

9. *Kollel* in *gematria* is an idea that one can add one to the sum of the letters representing the word as a whole.

Parshas Toldos

To be a Jew in All that We Do

ויצא הראשון אדמוני כלו כאדרת שער ויקראו שמו עשו: ואחרי־כן
יצא אחיו וידו אחזת בעקב עשו ויקרא שמו יעקב ויצחק בן־ששים
שנה בלדת אתם[1]

*The first one came out red with a full coat of hair, and they
called him Eisav. Afterwards, his brother came out clutching
the heel of Eisav, and he was called Yaakov. Yitzchak was sixty
years old when they were born.*

W<small>HEN PARENTS HAVE THE PRIVILEGE</small> to name a child
there is much contemplation and consideration prior to the decision. The name of a person captures one's essence and depth
and therefore requires wisdom and deliberation. The Midrash[2]
explains that even the Angels were unable to name the animals
and man. *Adam Harishon,* with insight and intelligence, was
able to name the animals, himself and even *Hashem.* Naming
is a talent gifted to man together with the help of divine influence from above. Many times when asking *Tzaddikim* for
advice concerning my own children, I was told to make sure to

---

1. *Parshas Toldos perek 25 pasukim 25-26*
2. *Bereishis Rabba 17:4.*

call my children by their complete name. The name of a person captures one's strengths and character traits and by hearing it reminds a person of one's abilities.

With these thoughts on the beauty and depth of a Jewish name, we will analyze the naming of our third Patriarch at the beginning of our *Parsha*. The Torah explains that Yaakov is given his name because he was born holding onto the *eikev*, heel, of his brother Eisav. This momentary occurrence seems like a superficial reason behind a name for life. What is the essence of Yaakov that was being captured by this name? According to one opinion in *Rashi*[3] this name was decided by *Hashem* himself. This knowledge requires even deeper explanation as a divinely determined name must have hidden meaning on a very deep level. Another important question arises as to why there is a letter *yud* added before the word *eikev*? Shouldn't Yaakov have just been called *eikev*? Although now that may sound strange, it is only because we are not accustomed to that name.

The name of Eisav also seems to be altered. *Rashi*[4] explains that the name Eisav represents the fact that he emerged as a finished product. This is clear from the *pasuk* as his body was full of hair. The *Shem Mishmuel*[5] explains that this was the essence of the negative character of Eisav. He always considered himself a finished product, not needing to work on himself or grow. This was the foundation that led him to his ways of wickedness. Just as Yaakov seems to have an added *yud*, Eisav is missing one from his end. The word for an object being finished would be *Assui* including a *yud* at the end. Where did this *yud* disappear to?

---

3. *Toldos, perek* 25, *pasuk* 26.
4. Ibid., *pasuk* 25.
5. *Shem Mishmuel, Parshas Vayeitze,* 5681.

The *Megaleh Amukos*[6] explains that Yaakov snatched this *yud* from the end of Eisav and placed it at his head. This is symbolized by the act of Yaakov grabbing onto the final heel of Eisav. He was seizing the last *yud* for himself.

This *yud* that clearly represents the *kedusha* of *Hashem*, as it is found at the beginning of the name of *Hashem*, at first is found at the end of Eisav. A relationship with *Hashem* was the last thing on Eisav's mind. Yaakov however wanted this to be his first priority.

Still why did Yaakov need to take this *yud* from Eisav, and what is the significance of adding it to the word Eikev?

When thinking about a *yud* being added to the beginning of a name, the immediate connection is made to Yehoshua. Yehoshua at first is named Hoshea and only in preparation to becoming one of the *meraglim* does Moshe add a *yud* to his name to help protect him. *Rashi*[7] explains that by adding a *yud*, Moshe was connecting this *yud* to the *hey* that already was there to form the name of *Hashem* at the beginning of Yehoshua's name.

What is the significance of this name that it would offer protection to Yehoshua?

The story of the *meraglim* has been debated for generations to understand how it could have occurred. After all, the *meraglim* were considered great leaders of *Bnei Yisrael*. How could it be possible that they would not want to enter into the holiest of lands to connect to *Hashem*? The Belzer Rebbi *ztz"l* explains[8] that the *meraglim* understood that once *Bnei Yisrael* entered *Eretz Yisrael* the miraculous existence of the desert life

6. *Parshas Toldos.*
7. *Parshas Shelach, perek* 13, *pasuk* 16.
8. *Shevelei Pinchas,* 5771, *Parshas Shelach.*

would end. No longer would the *mann* fall or their clothing grow with them. There would be a need to support oneself and be involved in a world of materialism that can easily pull one away from *ruchnius* and Torah study. The *meraglim* wanted no place in this new world and therefore suggested to stay in the desert.

The *meraglim* did not appreciate the *kedusha* found when materialism is elevated to a level of spirituality. They didn't understand that an *eved Hashem* is one who is able to connect to *Hashem* in all that they do and still find as much time as possible to learn the holy Torah. This is surely the world we all live in and this is our *tafkid*. To see *Hashem* in everything and connect to *ruchnius* every moment of life should be our goal. There is no need to abstain from all that is physical in order to achieve that level.

The *Gemara* in *Menachos*[9] explains that the world of *Olam Habba*, the world of only *ruchnius*, was created with the letter *yud*, and our world, the world of the physical, was created with the letter *hey*. Moshe added the letter *yud* to the letter *hey* of Yehoshua in order to illustrate to Yehoshua that unlike his fellow *meraglim,* he should not be afraid of entering into a physical world. One needs to attach the *yud* of *ruchnius* to the *hey* of the mundane and elevate everything in order to build a bond with *Hashem*.

This insight can explain why the name of *Hashem* found when combining *ish*, man, and *isha*, woman, in marriage is the name *Yud Hey*. The man brings the *yud* in his name of *ish* and places it next to the *hey* of the *isha*. This is symbolic of the couple who will *Bezras Hashem* lift up all of the physical world which occupies much of their focus to a level of spirituality.

---

9. *Menachos* 29b.

They will combine the *yud* of the spiritual to the *hey* of the mundane.

This was the message given to Yaakov as well, by attaching the same *yud* to the *eikev*. The *eikev* is the lowest part of the body, representing full physicality. Yaakov would be the first Jew to spend time in exile. Yaakov would succeed, as the essence that we see in his name was that he understood the importance of elevating all that is mundane in this world.[10]

The *Beis Halevi*[11] explains that this was the understanding that Rivkah had when telling Yaakov to steal the *brachos* from Eisav. Yitzchak thought that these *brachos* full of blessings in the physical should be accepted by Eisav so that Yaakov can be free to be fully involved in Torah. This was similar to the calculation of the *meraglim*. Rivkah understood that a true *Eved Hashem* can have it all and be successful. We need to elevate every area of our life to *Avodas Hashem*.

Yaakov took the *brachos* from Eisav as he originally took his *yud* from the end of his name!! Yaakov was able to epitomize the lesson behind the ladder he will see in next week's *parsha* that was standing on the ground, but reaching up to the heavens. Yaakov is the father of the entire Jewish nation as we are called *Bnei Yisrael*. We must learn from Yaakov how to raise every element of our lives to a level of holiness. There is nothing in this world that one does that is unable somehow to bring one closer to *Hashem*. We must realize that we can be successful and not retreat from this task.

*

The following story helped teach me this lesson:

Over the past few years, with the help of a very special friend

---

10. *Shevelei Pinchas*, 5771, *Parshas Shelach*.
11. *Beis Halevi, Parshas Toldos.*

and the devotion of my *Eishes Chayil*, I have been *zoche* to spend the holiest day of the year just a few steps away from the *makom* of the *Avodah* of Yom Kippur, davening with my special *talmidim* in Yeshivas Netiv Aryeh. Words cannot do justice to the beautiful *teffilos* or the feeling of being able to look up and stare at *Har Habayis* while reading the *Avodah* of the *Kohen Gadol* on that very spot.

The first year that I was privileged to find myself in Yerushalayim on Yom Kippur, I started a *minhag* I have kept up ever since. I make sure to prepare myself for Yom Kippur early in the day. This is actually not that difficult with my wife and children an ocean apart. I proceed to the Kossel to don my *kittel* and *tallis* and recite *Teffilas Zaka*. On that first year and every year since, the Kotel plaza has been almost completely empty as I daven outside in the corner closest to the entrance to the inside cave.

During that first year, as I was preparing for Yom Kippur with this powerful *teffilah*, I suddenly felt something hit my arm. I looked up and saw a beautiful dove sitting on a Kotel stone staring into my eyes. I braced for the worst and slowly looked down to view the damage. *Baruch Hashem* the droppings from the bird had hit off my arm and fell to the floor. There was not even a speck seen on my still white as a dove *kittel*. After looking back up to the heavens with a smile of *hakaras hatov* I looked back into my *machzor* to continue my *teffilos*.

The very next line that I was up to reciting was, *"We have removed from ourselves the holy image that garbs us . . . We have donned soiled clothing. How can we come to the gate of the King in sackcloth and clothing soiled with excrement?"* Could it be that the very line I was up to in my *machzor* was just played out in real life for me? I stopped and started to cry as I felt maybe this was a bad omen from the One Above. Within seconds the *Ribbono*

Shel Olam allowed a different appreciation of the situation to enter my mind. Being that there was no stain left on my clothing perhaps the message sent was that although the *Yetzer Hara* was trying, I was still, with the help of *Hashem*, staying clean. With that hope and wish I was able to dance into Yom Kippur with a positive sense of *Bitachon*.

We live in a physical world full of all forms of *tzoah* that can stain our pure *Neshama*. There is temptation towards that which pulls one away from *Hashem* not just in every direction we look, but often carried with us in our own pockets. We must believe in ourselves and our ability to elevate this world to live a life of *kedusha*, elevating the materialistic world to serve *Hashem*. We can keep our *Neshama* pure and white as a dove, and even polish it to a sparkling shine along the way.

Parshas Vayeitze

Even if Our Feet are on Earth our Head can be in *Shamayim*

ויצא יעקב מבאר שבע וילך חרנה: ויפגע במקום וילן שם כי־בא
השמש ויקח מאבני המקום וישם מראשתיו וישכב במקום ההוא:
ויחלם והנה סלם מצב ארצה וראשו מגיע השמימה והנה מלאכי
א־להים עלים וירדים בו[1]

*Yaakov left Beer Shevah and went to Charan. He reached
the place and slept there when the sun descended. He took the
stones of the place and surrounded his head and lied down
there. He dreamt that behold there was a ladder resting on
the ground and its top reached the heavens. And behold, there
were angels ascending and descending the ladder.*

To be successful as a *ben Torah* living in an immoral
and corrupt world is extremely difficult. Much energy must
be invested in order to position oneself in the most conducive
atmosphere possible to have a chance to succeed. It is not
merely our close family and friends that are able to influence
a person's actions, but the broader environment can affect the
way we conduct our actions. One who is surrounded by people

---

1. *Parshas Vayeitze, perek 28, pasukim 10–12.*

who are *bnei Torah* steeped in *midos tovos* and *amalus Betorah*, if only by osmosis, will lean towards their ways. The opposite is just as true. When a person finds himself amongst people who live immoral lives, focusing on everything except Torah and *mitzvos*, it is generally just a matter of time before he becomes just like them. The power of one's atmosphere cannot be underestimated. At the same time it is inevitable that at times one may find himself in a less than ideal surrounding and must not despair. We must realize that we have the tools and abilities to succeed in all places.

As we open up this week's *parsha,* this is the exact predicament in which we find Yaakov Avinu. He was in the holiest of atmospheres all his life, learning Torah under the guidance of his father and grandfather in *Eretz Yisrael.* Yaakov *Avinu* was a *talmid* of the *gedolim* Avraham, Yitzchak, Sheim, and Eiver until the age of 63. He only knew of the purest of environments and was successful as an *ish taam yosheiv ohalim.*

At the beginning of *Parshas Vayeitze,* Yaakov finds himself leaving this safe and holy location on the road to a location full of deceit and immorality. He is running away from Eisav who wants to kill him and heading towards his family in Charan where he hopes to find a wife. The Gemara in *Chulin*[2] explains that after reaching Charan, Yaakov realizes that he had forgotten to *daven* in the place where his ancestors *davened.* He didn't stop by *Har Habayis* to *daven* for his success in what will surely be a difficult situation. He decides he must turn back to *daven.* At this moment *Hashem* shortens the journey for Yaakov. In general, when we find such a miracle of *kefitzas haderech,* as we do when Eliezer travels to find a mate for Yitzchak, we observe that a journey that would usually take longer is accomplished

---

2. *Chulin* 91b.

in a small amount of time. Perhaps a weeklong journey would take only one day. Here, however, *Hashem* performs *kefitzas haderech* unlike any other place in the Torah. *Hashem* lifts up *Har Habayis* and brings it to Charan. Yaakov does not need to take one step forward, as *Hashem* brought his destination to him. Why perform such a revealed miracle in this particular instance? Why change the way journeys are expedited throughout the rest of the Torah?

The Midrash[3] says that when Yaakov reached Charan he was so anxious that it was as if there was a wall in front of him. He had such fear of living in an impure society and was hesitant to enter. How would he still be able to grow and develop a deeper relationship with The One Above living amongst wickedness? He would not be in Kansas anymore. He would no longer have the influences of Avraham, Yitzchak, Sheim or Eiver by his side. He would no longer feel the holiness of the land of *Eretz Yisrael* under his feet. How could he move on?

Rav Moshe Feinstein explains[4] that countering this mindset was exactly why *Hashem* brought *Har Habayis* to Charan. Yaakov was being taught that even here you can elevate this place to the holiness of *Har Habayis*. It is within your ability to be successful on the highest of levels even here in Charan, as if you are standing on *Har Habayis*. You don't need to have the perfect surroundings to thrive. It is up to you and not any external factor.

Rav Moshe himself was a true embodiment of this message. Rav Moshe chose to lead our nation in the land that was then referred to as the *midbar*, the desert, of America. He could have followed fellow *gedolim* to *Eretz Yisrael*, but understood he was

---

3. *Bereishis Rabba* 68:10.
4. *Drash Moshe, Parshas Vayeitze.*

needed in *chutz laaretz* and understood as well that he was able
to achieve equal heights there.

This was the message in Yaakov's dream of the ladder as
well. The base was resting on the ground as the peak reached
up into the heavens. We can be living in the most earthly of
places and still elevate our lives to the holiest existence. A person must not use their environment as an excuse, but always
strive to make the most of wherever he is found.

ויצו אתם לאמר כה תאמרון לאדני לעשו: כה אמר עבדך יעקב עם־
לבן גרתי ואחר עד־עתה:⁵

רש"י – גרתי ... דבר אחר גרתי בגימטריא תרי"ג, כלומר עם לבן
הרשע גרתי ותרי"ג מצות שמרתי ולא למדתי ממעשיו הרעים⁶

*He said to them tell my master Eisav that Yaakov said he has so-
journed with Lavan and waited until now.*

RASHI – *The word Garti (sojourn) in gematria is 613. Yaakov
was telling Eisav that although I have lived with the evil Lavan, I
have not been influenced by his ways. I have kept all the mitzvos.*

Yaakov was ultimately successful. For 20 years Yaakov lived
under the deceitful Lavan in Charan and stayed connected
to *Hashem.* He continued to grow and, with the birth of the
Shevatim, built the foundation for *Bnei Yisrael.* How was he able
to succeed? How are we able to succeed?

Rashi⁷ explains at the beginning of *Parshas Vayeitze* that
prior to reaching Charan, Yaakov stopped for 14 years in Yeshiva Sheim and Eiver to learn Torah. At the age of 63 when
told by his father that it is time to get married, Yaakov felt it
was first important to learn Torah for 14 additional years. For

5. *Parshas Vayishlach, perek 32, pasuk 5.*
6. *Rashi,* ibid.
7. *Parshas Vayeitze, perek 28, pasuk 11.*

these 14 years, as pointed out by Rashi, he never lied down to sleep. Yaakov understood that there was only one means of protection to enable him to be successful in a bad environment. The light of Torah would be his driving force and he therefore needed that foundation to be rock solid.

The holy Torah is the same in every environment. *Maseches Baba Kamma* is the same *Baba Kamma* in Bnei Brak and New York City. It is the same *Baba Kamma* in Yerushalayim as it was hidden in communist Russia by some holy angels. It is the same *Baba Kamma* in Beis Medrash Gavoah of Lakewood as is found in a Chabad in Hawaii. With Torah by our side we are armed with the ability to fight against any and all negative influences.

Torah is the ladder that connects *Eretz* and *Shamayim*. This is hinted to in the very image of a ladder. The *Gematria* of *Sulam* is 130. This is the exact *Gematria* of *Sinai*. The Torah given at *Har Sinai* is the medium given to us by *Hashem* in order to connect this world to the heaven above. Even the most unholy of places can be elevated to *kedusha* with the filter of Torah. The ascending and descending angels in the dream of Yaakov also express this idea. The words *malachei Elokim olim veyordim* are 607 in *gematria*. This is the exact *Gematria* to the *millui* of *emes*. Emes is the *Toras Emes*. The ability to ascend this ladder connecting our world to the world of Torah is *Toras Emes*. One must never fall into despair in a difficult environment. We must remind ourselves that we are children of Yaakov who can always succeed with Torah at our side.

*

The following story describes a situation where holiness was achieved in the most unholy of places. In *Mitzrayim* we fell to the lowest of levels, but in this instance, that same place was the stage for bringing the *Shechina* and the *Malach Refael* into our world.

A little over 2 years ago the *Olam Haemes* gained a true *Tzaddik* taken from our midst. Dr. Joshua Feibush was a constantly growing *eved Hashem* in the area of *Bein Adam Lemakom* as well as a hidden *Tzaddik* in *Bein Adam Lechaveiro*. A book filled with stories of his life would be an incredibly inspiring work for us all. His son, Chaim Gedalya, is a very close *talmid* of mine and therefore I was lucky enough to have absorbed some of the *kedusha* of Dr. Feibush.

Late in 2006, Dr Feibush was diagnosed with a very serious cancer. The doctors in Sloan Kettering said those horrifying words – that there is nothing more they can do. Dr. Feibush had been in remission for years after having one lung removed due to cancer. Now the horrible disease was threatening his life once again. He decided to travel to Pittsburgh to experiment with about 6 rounds of experimental chemotherapy on a clinical trial. Despite unfavorable odds, Dr. Feibush continued to persevere.

January of 2007, I was in Eretz Yisrael visiting my *talmidim* learning in *yeshivos*. Late Tuesday night, I was meeting with Harav Aharon Bina the *Rosh Yeshiva* of Yeshiva Netiv Aryeh where Chaim Gedalya spent the previous year. Harav Bina happens to have a very close relationship with the great *mekubal* Rebbe Dovid Abuchatzeira. I brought Rav Bina up to date on the situation of Dr. Feibush and asked him if he could somehow receive a *bracha* on his behalf from Rebbe Dovid.

Rav Bina assured me that he already knew how serious the case was and proceeded to pull out a card full of names. He showed me Dr. Feibush's name and told me he personally davens for him every *teffilah*. He then told me that two days prior, he traveled with Rebbe Dovid to Egypt to visit the grave of Rebbe Yaakov Abuchatzeira, Rebbe Dovid's ancestor, on the yahrzeit of the Abir Yaakov. While there, he gave Rebbe Dovid the name of Dr. Feibush. Rebbe Dovid then did *hishtatchus*[8] on the kever and *davened* for his *refuah*. I walked away from that update with a sense of calm and a touch of cautious hope.

The next Sunday morning I landed back in New York and that night called my *talmid* to tell him about the *teffilos* from Rebbe Dovid. Before I could say a word my *talmid* told me the amazing news. His father returned back home, as midway thru his experimental treatments the doctors performed a scan and miraculously all was clear. With a feeling of tremendous *simcha* I asked him when that scan revealing the miracle had been performed. Exactly a week ago, this past Sunday, was his answer – the very same day that Rebbe Dovid *davened* for him by the Abir Yaakov.

In *Mitzrayim*, the place of a treacherous exile, Rebbe Dovid pulled out sparks of *kedusha*. We must pull out the sparks of *kedusha* wherever we are.

---

8. *Hishtatchus* is a method of lying on the grave of a tzaddik in order to connect to the soul of the tzaddik.

Parshas Vayishlach

You Are Never Alone

ויותר יעקב לבדו ויאבק איש עמו עד עלות השחר[1]
Yaakov was left alone and a man fought with him until dawn.

AFTER GRADUATING HIGH SCHOOL I experienced the life
altering privilege of learning Torah in Eretz Yisrael at Yeshivas
Kerem Byavneh. I look back at those years of growth in *limud
Hatorah* and *Avodas Hashem* as the most formative years of my
life. I would be remiss if I did not state that much of my devel-
opment is owed to my Rebbe, Harav Mendel Blachman. Prior
to my second year in Yeshivah I decided to spend the summer
as a *madrich* on NCSY Kollel, a summer learning program for
teenage boys situated in *Eretz Yisrael*. That awe inspiring summer helped pave my path towards a career in *chinuch*. Being
that the summer program ended a few days before Rosh Cho-
desh Ellul, I was one of the first *talmidim* to arrive in Yeshivah
for the *zman* of Ellul 5757. Leading up to Yeshivah, I recall
feelings of anticipation and excitement to return to learning a
full day again. Those feelings were quickly altered for the few
days that I found myself in Yeshivah with practically nobody

---

1. *Parshas Vayishlach, perek 32, pasuk 25.*

else there. I can sadly recall feelings of loneliness and a loss of yearning to excel. I started to build the desire to be anywhere else. My emotions caused me to question whether I should be in this Yeshiva, although I quickly realized my loneliness was creating a false perception of reality. I was unable to deal with being alone, and until my friends began to join me in Yeshivah I suffered greatly. As Yeshiva began to fill, these feelings all dissipated, and I enjoyed a meaningful *zman* of growth. I did however personally learn the pains of loneliness that I don't wish upon anyone. In order to feel happy and be productive, one can never feel alone. The truth is, when one realizes *Hashem* is always by our side there is never room for loneliness.

Perhaps this glimpse into one difficult moment of my life can help to understand one of the strangest episodes in *Sefer Bereishis*. After Yaakov *Avinu* has built our nation while working for his father-in-law Lavan in *Charan*, he is finally ready to return to *Eretz Yisrael*. Prior to transitioning to the next stage in his life, old troubles must be revisited. Yaakov realizes that he must face his brother and nemesis Eisav. Yaakov prepares for this meeting in many ways and ultimately emerges unscathed.

On his way to meeting his brother, Yaakov has a very unusual encounter. He wrestles with, and ultimately defeats, the *malach* of Eisav. Surely this spiritual brawl is on some level a foreshadowing of the success Yaakov will enjoy when finally meeting his brother in person. Yet at the same time, we are forced to wonder what gave the *malach* the capability to rise against Yaakov and to ultimately damage Yaakov and inflict a terrible blow to Yaakov's thigh, his *gid hanashe,* leaving him maimed. How was the *malach* able to harm the *tzaddik* who was our pillar of Torah, Yaakov *Avinu*?

The answer I would like to share I can only write because it is not my own. In general, it is very hard for anyone to talk about the detriments of one of our *Avos*, a person who on our greatest of days, we couldn't even aspire to reach his heels. Only because I read these words from a great *Tzaddik* can I offer this idea. The great student of the Baal Shem Tov known as the Toldos Yaakov Yosef[2] suggests that the opening *pasuk* to this encounter has buried within it the explanation as to why the angel was able to fight with Yaakov and even achieve some level of success in that battle.

Only after "*Vayivasser Yaakov levado,*" Yaakov was left alone, are we introduced to "*Vayeavek ish imo,*" that a man fought with him. Yaakov, for these few moments of life, was alone and therefore vulnerable to be hurt by this *malach*. Yaakov for a short time was not just physically alone from other people, but alone from Hashem, allowing himself to collapse and be damaged.

All destruction in life occurs when we are alone and most specifically alone from *Hashem*. This was the message being taught by this most unusual occurrence. When *Hashem* is by our side one understands all is good both in spirituality and in the physical world. When we feel distanced from *Hashem,* we become exposed to harm in all types of ways. Even if we are passing through a difficult time in life, if *Hashem* is felt by our side there is no depression or panic.

As Dovid Hamelech taught us

גם כי־אלך בגיא צלמות לא־אירא רע כי־אתה עמדי[3]

Even as I walk in the valley of darkness I have no fear because You are with me.

As I like to say – when one is with *Hashem,* all is good!!

---

2. *Toldos Yaakov Yosef, parshas Vayishlach 7.*

3. *Tehillim, perek 23, pasuk 4.*

With this idea in mind a Midrash in Eicha can be understood.

אלו זכיתם הייתם קוראים בתורה (דברים א') איכה אשא לבדי,
ועכשיו שלא זכיתם הרי אתם קוראים איכה ישבה בדד[4]

*If we are worthy we would read in the Torah, "How can I bear
alone?" Now that we are not worthy we read, "How can it sit
alone?"*

It makes a lot of sense for the Midrash to state that as long as
we do not merit the *geulah* we will still sit on the floor on *Tisha
B'Av* and read *Eicha Yashva Badad*. However, the first portion
of the Midrash is puzzling. What does it mean that if we merit
the *geulah* we will say "*Eicha essa levadi*"? This line from *Parshas
Devarim* was Moshe's complaint to *Hashem* that he could not
handle the needs of *Bnei Yisrael* alone. In what way is that a
symbol of *geulah*?

The *Zohar* in *Vayishlach* teaches that the first significant
event that occurred on *Tisha B'Av* night was not, as most of
us are taught, the story of the *meraglim*, but rather the fight
between Yaakov and the *Sar* of Eisav. Rav Tzaddok teaches that
the first occurrence of an event in history and in the Torah is
by definition the archetype for all such similar future events.
If one understands the deeper nature of this struggle, it sheds
light on the root causes of Exile.

As the Toldos Yaakov Yosef explained, the ability for the
malach to harm Yaakov was based on the loneliness that Yaakov
experienced, feeling distant from the One Above. So too, it is
clear that the foundation for any destruction for *Bnei Yisrael*
will always be based on feeling alone, far away from *Hashem*.
This loneliness is the underlying foundation of *Tisha B'Av* and
all *galus*.

---

4. *Midrash Eicha Rabba* 11

The Midrash is telling us that we have not yet been able to merit the *geulah* because we still feel alone on some level. We feel *Eicha yashva badad*, how do we sit in solitude, as we decide to continue to sit in solitude. We will only be *zoche* to *geulah* when we are ready to say *Eicha essa levadi*, I cannot bear to stay alone. We can't continue to sit in solitude, but need to be close with *Hashem* always and never again feel alone.

Anytime a person strays even in the slightest ways from *Torah umitzvos*, it is somehow based on a lack of *emunah*. At that moment of weakness, one is lacking belief that *Hashem* is watching this very moment and there will be consequences for his actions. In the most inspiring of ways the Ramban[5] explains the opinion of the *Behag*, that *emunah* is not counted as one of the 613 *mitzvos*. *Emunah* is not counted as one of the *mitzvos* because it lies at the heart of every individual *mitzvah*. Every *mitzvah* I keep or don't is dependent on my *emunah*. *Emunah* is not merely to believe that there is a force that created the world and gave us Torah. *Emunah* means I believe *Hashem* is with me every moment of my life.

When a person begins to live with this level of *emunah,* one will experience a life of constant *simcha*. As Harav Pam used to say, "We are all looking for the city of happiness, but must realize it is found in the state of mind." Realizing and feeling *Hashem* stands by one's side always is surely the state of mind Rav Pam was reffering to. When one walks with *Hashem* then *Lo ira ra ki ata imadi*. The sadness of *Tisha B'Av* is only brought into the world when we preempt the *gallus* with our own feelings of being separated from *Hashem*.

*

---

5. *Ramban* on the *Rambam Sefer Hamitzvos, mitzvah* 1.

The following story perhaps indirectly illustrates this idea. *Rashi*, based on the *Sifrei*,[6] explains that while the *pasuk* seems to command us to literally cling to *Hashem* in a physical capacity, that is obviously not possible. Therefore we are taught that in order to feel that connection with *Hashem*, we should first cling to the *tzaddikim* that are already so close to *Hashem*. This closeness to *Hashem* that one can glean from relationships to *Rabbeim* and *Tzaddikim* can be accomplished also posthumously near the *Kevarim* of *Tzaddikim*. The *Gemara*[7] tells us that *Tzaddikim* are considered spiritually alive even after death. There is also a part of the *nefesh* that stays connected to the body in this world.[8] There is much debate concerning how to *daven* by *Kivrei Tzaddikim*, but there is no doubt that *Kivrei Tzaddikim* are conducive places to feel the closeness we are yearning for with the One Above, and to help eradicate loneliness. It therefore is perfectly sensible that *Kivrei Tzaddikim* are often the setting at which *geulah* and *yeshuah* can be achieved by drawing nearer to *Hashem*.

One of the biggest *brachos* to be living in the Five Towns is dwelling about a 12 minute drive from the Ohel of the Lubavitcher Rebbe, Rav Menachem Mendel Schneerson, who is buried next to his father in law, the previous Rebbe, Rav Yosef Yitzchak. To daven by *Kivrei Tzaddikim* is *bechinas* davening in *Chevron* by *Maaras Hamachpeilah*,[9] and anyone who has been

---

6. *Parshas Eikev, perek* 11, *pasuk* 22.

7. *Brachos* 18a.

8. *Kuntres Hahishtatchus* by the Mittler Rebbe of Chabad from the teachings of the Arizal in *Likkutei Torah, Taamei Hamitzvos, Parshas Vayechi.*

9. *Kuntres Hishtatchus,* who also explains that the opening to *Gan Eden* is found there, and all *Teffilos* ascend from the entrance to *Gan Eden.*

to the Ohel surely has felt this. There is hardly a week that I don't find myself there davening for someone in need or just to gain much needed *chizuk*. Obviously such a holy place has many miraculous stories connected to it. Here is one personal story.

A few years ago Yaakov and Rachel[10] arrived at my house on a Thursday night looking for *eitzah* and comfort. About 2 years prior doctors found a benign tumor in Rachel's stomach that *Baruch Hashem* was treated successfully. Rachel and Yaakov now were married for a few months and again Rachel started to feel pains in her stomach. After dismissing it for awhile, she visited her doctor and her worst fears were realized. Rachel was told that she had a massive tumor in her lower stomach and they would have to operate as soon as possible. The doctor was unsure of whether it was cancerous and would not know until the tumor was removed. Rachel was also told that this was the reason she still was not pregnant and would surely not be able to conceive with a tumor in that location.

The young couple sat in my den in tears telling me the details of the unfortunate diagnosis. I tried my best to give as much *chizuk* as possible. After I felt that I said everything that my heart was telling me to relay and saw calm in their eyes, I walked them to the door with words of *bracha*. As they were leaving I told them that the next morning on *Erev Shabbos,* I would take my shiur to The Ohel and have every *talmid* daven on her behalf. That is exactly what was done the next morning. About 15 seniors in high school poured out their hearts at The Ohel to bring a *refuah* for Rachel.

The next Monday night I received a call from Yaakov in an elated voice. He relayed to me how that morning they met

---

10. Names have been changed.

with the doctor to be briefed on the procedures prior to the operation scheduled for the upcoming Wednesday. The doctor decided to do a sonogram to check the tumor one final time. To the amazement of the doctor he could not find any tumor at all. The massive growth had miraculously disappeared and the doctor had no explanation.

It was less than a year later that Rachel gave birth to her first healthy and beautiful child. The doctor may have had no explanation, but I have no doubt that the emotional prayers at The Ohel brought *yeshuah and refuah* into the world. My *talmidim* for those moments felt very close to *Hashem*, creating an opportunity for *geulah*.

Parshas Vayeishev

One Can Change

וישב ראובן אל־הבור והנה אין־יוסף בבור ויקרע את־בגדיו[1]
Reuven returned to the pit and Yosef was no longer in the pit.
He therefore tore his clothing.

IMAGINE FOR A MOMENT a universe without the ability to do *teshuvah*. What joy would we be able to experience during our journey of life if one would be forced to live with one's past mishaps perpetually on our minds. Some of the greatest Jews in our history such as Rabbi Akiva have been *Baalei Teshuvah*, and all of us on some level I hope consider ourselves *Baalei Teshuvah*. Imagine a world with no potential for the cleansing of a Yom Kippur, a world with no ability to fix a regrettable mistake. The world would probably be a very somber place to live. One of the greatest gifts from *Hashem* is the gift of *teshuvah*. *Hashem*, as *Rashi*[2] points out at the beginning of *Bereishis* created the world not merely with *din*, judgement, but with *rachamim*, mercy. We have the chance to fix our past and perform *teshuvah*. In fact, the Zohar points out that *teshuvah* was

---

1. *Parshas Vayeishev, perek 37, pasuk 29.*
2. *Parshas Bereishis, perek 1, pasuk 1.*

even created before the world itself. *Hashem* understands that the prerequisite for us to live a meaningful and enjoyable life is to have the potential to repair our past.

It seems that so few avail themselves of this gift. For many the task often seems too vast and daunting. Many believe that the only way to achieve *teshuvah* is to completely change every aspect of one's life. One would need to alter any wrongdoings until one is perfect in all facets of *Avodas Hashem*. While such a level of *teshuvah* is surely admirable and ultimately desired by *Hashem*, it is not the only path. One must not become discouraged from even the smallest level of *teshuvah* and must try to improve in even the slightest of ways.

The Midrash[3] teaches that when Reuven returned to the pit to pull his brother Yosef out, he was performing the first act of *teshuvah* in the Torah. Reuven understood that the act he partook in of throwing Yosef into the pit was wrong and potentially fatal. He returned to repair the wrongdoing and help his younger brother. According to the Midrash, in all of history prior to Reuven, no person made a mistake and decided to fix the act.

Seemingly, one can question the authenticity of the teaching of this Midrash. Is this really the first case of *teshuvah* in the Torah? Didn't Kayin beg for forgiveness after killing Hevel?[4] Didn't Adam perform teshuvah after eating from the *Eitz Hadaas*?[5] What does the Midrash mean that Reuven was the first in history to carry out *teshuvah*?

When I was a junior in High School attending MTA I heard the most beautiful elucidation of this Midrash from

---

3. *Bereishis Rabba* 84:19.
4. *Bereishis Rabba* 22:13.
5. *Eiruvin* 18b.

Harav Binyomin Yudin. Let us review the storyline of what led to the throwing of Yosef into the pit. The brothers who despised Yosef wanted him dead. They were prepared to kill him and rid themselves of their aggravation. Reuven, the oldest brother, had sympathy and was able to convince his brothers to throw him in a pit instead. To save him altogether, he realized, was too large of a request from the mob of his brothers. He therefore felt at the time the best he could do was to save him from death and suggest the severe punishment of being left in a pit. After leaving the scene to care for his father Yaakov, Reuven returns to pull Yosef out of the pit. Reuven knew that although he did a virtuous act by convincing his brothers not to kill, it was not good enough. Reuven contemplated his act of good and decided to try to improve upon that act.

There were definitely others such as Kayin and Adam that did *teshuvah* prior to Reuven. They succeeded in performing the classical form of *teshuvah*, fixing something they did wrong. Reuven, on the other hand, had the privilege of being the first to initiate a new form of *teshuvah* in the world. He was the first person to do *teshuvah* on a *mitzvah*. Reuven was the first in history to take a positive act and scrutinize it in order to improve that action. This is what the Midrash means when it asserts that Reuven was the first to attain *teshuvah* in our world. He was the first to do *teshuvah* on a *mitzvah*.

For some people it is very difficult to uproot an act that is being done wrong. It is hard to change one's bad habits, and tough to defeat temptation and laziness. Inertia prevails to just give up and continue on in the same way. Sometimes it may be easier and therefore more worthwhile to begin our improvement in our relationship with *Hashem* by taking the *mitzvos* we are already doing and decide to do them better. We can improve our *kavannah* and improve how meticulous we are about a particular *mitzvah* we already perform.

For some, even suggesting improving our positive *mitzvos* seems like a task too large to handle. Can I really improve my *kavannah* in davening? Is it possible to toil in learning the way I did during my years in Yeshivah? One of my favorite pieces of Torah from Harav Pam[6] explaining the final *Mishna* in *Meseches Yoma* can add another element of hope to becoming a *Baal Teshuva*.

אמר רבי עקיבא אשריכם ישראל לפני מי אתם מיטהרין מי מטהר
אתכם אביכם שבשמים שנאמר וזרקתי עליכם מים טהורים וטהרתם
ואומר מקוה ישראל ה' מה מקוה מטהר את הטמאים אף הקדוש
ברוך הוא מטהר את ישראל[7]

Rabbi Akivah said, "Praiseworthy are Bnei Yisrael because they are purified by Hashem. This is learned from the following two pasukim. "I will sprinkle on you purifying waters and you will be pure." "The mikveh of Bnei Yisrael is Hashem." Just as a mikveh purifies those who are impure, so does Hashem purify Yisrael.

Why is it that the great sage Rabbi Akiva felt it necessary to quote two *pasukim* to prove that *Hashem* purifies us from our wrongdoings. There are obviously many examples in the Torah, and seemingly Rabbi Akiva only needed to bring one *pasuk*. What message was the *Tanna* trying to teach by citing both of these specific *pasukim*?

The two waters, the waters of a *mikveh* and the waters being sprinkled, are two very distinct forms of purification. The water of a *mikveh* can only bring purity if every drop of the person is immersed under the water. If even one little finger is sticking

---

6. *Attara Lemelech*, p. 173.
7. *Yoma, perek 8, mishna* 9.

out of the pool of water the *mikveh* has no effect. The Rambam[8] explains that the sprinkling water of the *parah adumah* being brought in the other *pasuk* is exactly the opposite. The impure individual need not be splashed all over for the water to take effect. If the water is merely sprinkled on one little finger the person gains purity.

Rabbi Akiva is teaching every member of *Bnei Yisrael* that there are two ways to gain purity and to improve in our *Avodas Hashem*. We can jump into a *mikveh* with every aspect of our life being immersed and purified. We can become a new being in every area of serving *Hashem* and perform *teshuvah* in the highest of forms. However, for those of us who for the time being are unable to reach so high, there is another path towards purity. Take a little water and sprinkle on one area. Just change one little area of your life and a level of purity will be gained as well. Taking even one small deed and improving it qualifies a person as a *baal teshuvah*.

We should all aspire to greatness, and want to jump into a *mikveh* to become pure in every aspect of our life. We should want to uproot any slight deviation from serving *Hashem* and strive to be one with *Hashem* always. Unfortunately, there are those who if they tried to jump into a *mikveh,* will only end up drowning in the despair of failure. Not only will the goal of complete change not be reached, but the failure can create a feeling of lowliness, losing all desire for any improvement.

The Torah teaches us that we can follow in the footsteps of Reuven and start our journey of growth by looking to improve the good we already do. And even in our striving to improve the good, we do not need to make dramatic changes right away. We can sprinkle the purifying waters on one small area at a

---

8. *Mishna Torah, Hilchos Parah Adumah, perek 12, halacha 1.*

time and take small steps closer to *Hashem*. If we continue to sprinkle constantly, eventually we will find ourselves soaked as if we had jumped into the *mikveh*.

If we follow this formula of *teshuvah* we can fulfill the *pasukim* that the Ramban explains referring to *teshuvah*.

כי המצוה הזאת אשר אנכי מצוך היום לא־נפלאת הוא ממך ולא
רחקה הוא: לא בשמים הוא לאמר מי יעלה־לנו השמימה ויקחה לנו
וישמענו אתה ונעשנה: ולא־מעבר לים הוא לאמר מי יעבר־לנו אל־
עבר הים ויקחה לנו וישמענו אתה ונעשנה: כי־קרוב אליך הדבר מאד
בפיך ובלבבך לעשתו[9]

This mitzvah that I have commanded you today is not too much of a wonder or too far. It is not up in heaven that one needs to say, "Who will go up to heaven to take it for us so that we could keep it?" It is not on the other side of the sea that we need to say, "Who will cross the sea to take it for us so that we could keep it?" It is very close. You have the ability in your mouth and heart to perform it.

It can be done and is not too difficult.

*

The following story is one small example of being able to perform a small act of *teshuvah* in a special way.

One of the most amazing and inspiring gathering of *Yidden* during any given year is *Lag B'omer* in Meiron by the *Kever* of Rav Shimon Bar Yochai. Only if you have been there do you truly understand the feeling of *davening* and dancing together with hundreds of thousands of *Yidden* from all walks of life. The experience has been described to be as joyous as *Simchas Torah* outside the *Kever*, and as inspirational as Yom Kippur inside.

On *Lag B'omer* 2008, together with Rabbi Eli Brazil and 17

---

9. *Parshas Netzavim, perek* 30, *pasukim* 11 and 14.

talmidim, I had the *zchus* to be present at *Kever Rashbi*. I still
live daily with the *chizuk* of that night and will never forget
how special it was. *Lag B'omer* is the yahrzeit of Reb Shimon
Bar Yochai, one of our greatest *tanaim,* and source of the Torah
in the holy Zohar. He was one of the 5 *talmidim* that Rabbi
Akiva taught starting on *Lag B'omer* after his 24,000 Talmidim
perished during the days of *Sefiras Haomer*. He who can truly
understand the depth of this special day would only be one
who understands the depth of the *Kabbalah* of Reb Shimon,
but anyone who has been there feels it in the air.

On our inspirational excursion we arrived in *Eretz Yisrael* on
a Thursday afternoon after a week of visiting the holy *Kivrei
Tzaddikim* in the Ukraine. We immediately drove straight up
to Tzfat to drop off our belongings, and from there to Meiron,
arriving on *Lag B'omer* at about 11 pm. The plan was to go to
the top of the mountain and to first daven *maariv* together,
and then enjoy the night of *teffilah* and *tantzing*. Yehudah
Aryeh Mazel and Asher Chaim Gleitman were so amazed
by the scene and excited to be a part of the *simcha* that they
asked if they can opt out of our minyan and *daven* later. Since
there would be *minyanim* throughout the night the request was
granted and they were off to *tantzing*.

About 4:30 am I meet up with these 2 *talmidim* outside the
Kever. They were so excited to share every moment of their
amazing and inspirational night. I proceeded to ask them if
they remembered to *daven Maariv* as they did not *daven* in our
minyan. Being so caught up in the excitement of the night
they had completely forgotten. I quickly calculated that the
time right then was in between *alos hashachar,* dawn, and *neitz
hachama*, sunrise. Most *Tzaddikim* are of the opinion that one
can not *daven maariv* at this time, as we have already crept into
daytime. The one *Tanna* who holds one can still *daven* is Reb

Shimon Bar Yochai!![10] Also, the Gemara[11] in *Brachos* explains "*Kedai Lismoch al Reb Shimon beshaas hadchak,*" one can rely on Reb Shimon in an urgent situation. I relayed both of these ideas to my *talmidim* and pointed to the *Kever* of Reb Shimon. I told them that being next to Reb Shimon on his day, you have who to rely upon. The two young men then *davened* the final *maariv* on *Lag B'omer* based on the *psak* of Reb Shimon.

We should always be looking to perform small acts of *teshuvah* that will add up to transforming ourselves into the *Tzaddikim* we know we can be.

---

10. *Brachos* 8b.
11. *Brachos* 9a.

Parshas Mikeitz

A King is Only Focused on His Kingdom

ויאמר פרעה אל־יוסף חלום חלמתי ופתר אין אתו ואני שמעתי עליך
לאמר תשמע חלום לפתר אתו[1]

*Pharoah said to Yosef, "I have dreamt a dream and it has not
been interpreted. I have heard about you that if you listen to a
dream you can interpret it."*

ARGUABLY THE MOST EXCITING night of one's life is that
of one's wedding. The emotions of a fresh beginning of a life
with a spouse you yearn to build a home with is uplifting and
inspiring. We all look forward to that night and many have in
some way planned for those few hours their entire life. Obviously more important than a beautiful *chuppah* and a fun night
of dancing is what will begin when the lights in the hall dim.
This night is the beginning of the remainder of one's life. This
is the start of a family and new responsibility. There is no question that aside from preparing for the wedding itself, much
groundwork must be covered in preparation of marriage. Not
only must the new *mitzvos* that will be practiced need to be
learned, but an entirely new way of life must be understood.

---

1. *Parshas Mikeitz, perek* 41, *pasuk* 15.

Life as a single individual is radically different than that with a spouse. It is surely incumbent upon any engaged individual to seek counseling and advice in order to create a successful life of peace and harmony, as they do not truly have any understanding of what they are getting into.

Together with the depth of *Chazal* and an idea taken from our *Parsha,* I would like to share the most important foundation I try to pass on to every *chosson* and *kallah* I have the privilege to meet with before their marriage.

Pirkei Derabi Eliezer[2] famously teaches that a *chosson* is compared to a king. It would therefore surely follow that a bride is comparable to a queen. What is *Chazal* trying to teach in this comparison? Of course the immediate lesson is to teach how a bride and groom should treat each other. A spouse should always be treated as royalty and then surely your house will shine with tranquility.

It has also been suggested that the Midrash is suggesting to family and friends how to treat this new couple. The guests at a wedding should consider the couple as royalty. The guests therefore stand for them, dance in front of them and converse with the couple in the sweetest of ways.

Is there still a deeper foundation of marriage to be gleaned from this famous comparison?

Our *parsha* begins with the two dreams that are dreamt by King Pharoah. There are dreams of cows and dreams of wheat. Yosef, after interpreting the dreams of the butler and baker, is called on to interpret these dreams. Yosef explains that there will be seven years of plenty and seven years of famine. Pharoah accepts this elucidation and lauds Yosef as a wise man full of spirituality. On the spot he is appointed as Viceroy, in

2. *Perek* 16.

command of the entire palace. Yosef was not the first person to have heard and interpreted Pharoah's dreams. Prior to Yosef, the dreams were told to the Egyptian necromancers.

Rashi explains[3] that the necromancers said that the dreams were foreshadowing seven daughters that Pharoah would father and then bury. These Egyptians were the very individuals who Pharoah had trusted his entire life. Although their interpretation would be hard to swallow, why suddenly did Pharoah not trust their ideas, and accepted the perspective of a jailed Jew in their place? Of course Yosef did have success with the baker and butler, but wouldn't Pharoah trust his own advisors first?

Rav Zalman Sorotzkin in his *sefer Aznoyim LeTorah* explains[4] this decision of King Pharoah. Pharoah, being the king, believed that any dream he dreamt would not merely be meant on a personal level, but for his entire kingdom. As a king he dreams for all his people and not just for himself. The interpretation of the necromancers had implications for him personally, but not for his nation. Pharoah therefore understood that this could not be the message of his dream. The interpretation of Yosef, however, carried a message for his entire kingdom, which he felt must be correct.

This is perhaps the deeper lesson behind a *chosson* being compared to a king. Until one is engaged, a person can have their own personal goals and aspirations. A person makes decisions based on what he wants for his own future. The moment one commits to marriage, that all changes. No longer is there an "I" in life, only "We." Every goal and every aspiration is no longer about oneself, but concerns one's spouse as well. Every

---

3. *Parshas Mikeitz, perek* 41, *pasuk* 8.
4. Ibid.

decision bears the mindset of what is best for us and not just for me. The moment a person is engaged, a sense of royalty is gained as a kingdom to care for has been acquired. This is the foundation of what leads to a house full of peace and happiness. A married couple must only think about their kingdom and never themselves.

With this idea in mind the first words of *Maseches Kiddushin*[5] can be understood. The opening words of the tractate that deals with marriage are *haisha niknas*, a women is acquired. Referring to the ways that a man and woman can become halachically engaged, the Torah tells us a woman is acquired. To many this seems extremely chauvinistic and the complete opposite of what marriage should be about. Does a man acquire his wife as he would a maidservant?

I believe the Torah is actually teaching something very special about how a spouse should be treated. If a person saved a large sum of money to acquire something very special, it would be treated with the utmost care. If a person saved for years to purchase diamond earrings, the earrings would be watched over and protected in the finest of ways. The earrings would be kept locked in a safe and polished often. Much time and effort would be put into the care of the expensive acquisition.

This is what the *Mishna* is teaching every married man. You have just acquired the most precious item in the world. Make sure to care for your acquisition in the most special of ways.

This foundation of a marriage, of always focusing on one's spouse and placing their needs first, can also help explain a famous *Gemara* in *Sotah*.[6] The *Gemara* explains that bringing

---

5. *Kiddushin* 2a.
6. *Sotah* 2a.

together a *Shidduch* by *Hashem* is as difficult as it was to split the Red Sea when leaving *Mitzrayim*.

On its surface this is a very difficult *gemara* to understand. Why is it that *Krias Yam Suf* is compared to *Shidduchim*? In addition, what does it mean that something is difficult for The One Above?

Imagine the scene at *Krias Yom Suf*. Over two million people are leaving 210 years of residence in *Mitzrayim* and are suddenly stopped by the sea in front of them. At this very moment they turn around to view the Egyptians on horses and chariots running after them with death in their eyes. Suddenly the sea opens up. Imagine what pandemonium should have occurred. There should have been pushing, shoving, and trampling to save one's life and cross the sea. There should have been deaths and injuries with the rush toward safety across the sea. There are no such occurrences recorded anywhere. All of *Bnei Yisrael* was able to cross the sea in peace to safety. How did this happen? Every Jew needed to care about each other and pass as one unit. No Jew was able to selfishly worry about themselves at the expense of others. There was an orderly passing because each one exhibited empathy for another. This immense care for others displayed at the sea is often unnatural. This is what was so difficult about the crossing of the sea. Not the miracle on *Hashem's* part of splitting the sea, but the unified crossing of *Am Yisrael*.

This is the same root of what is so difficult regarding a *Shidduch*. Two people from two very different backgrounds with two sets of goals and aspirations decide to fuse together as one. In marriage there needs to be the same degree of empathy and mutual understanding as that of *Krias Yam Suf*. Care needs to be shown toward a spouse, and one's own needs placed on hold. Although that is a difficult transition to make, it is indispensible for a healthy marriage full of joy and tranquility.

Of course prior to putting all of these ideas into practice one must first find one's *bashert*. Often that can be a long and draining journey. One must always have *emunah* and *bitachon* that *Hashem* has a plan. I often tell my students that dating is not a race. If I could tell you that you could get married in six months to a spouse who will just be average and lead to an average marriage, or you can wait four years and have the most unbelievable marriage full of *simcha*, *bracha* and *shalom*, which would you choose? The *gemara* teaches us that after creating the world *Hashem* has been constantly involved in *shidduchim*. *Hashem* is by our side making sure we will have a special marriage. Don't stop believing.

*

The following story can hopefully be a *chizuk* to those who are still waiting for their *bashert*, and are often saddened when a dating situation ends.

A few years ago on a Thursday night I received a phone call from a *talmid* who sounded very down on the other end. He had been dating a young woman and felt that things were progressing very nicely. It was only about six dates into the relationship, but he was very excited about the potential. Shockingly the young woman ended the relationship. The young man was very taken aback, as usually one has a good sense for how the other feels by that point of the dating process. Every date seemed to have gone very nicely.

I gave him *chizuk* for a while in *emunah* and *bitachon*. He seemed to have been doing a little better by the time we got off the phone, and I knew with time he would be fine.

That *Leil Shabbos* the Rebbe where I daven, Harav Dovid Spiegel, shared a Torah that I knew this Talmid had to hear. It was the Torah behind all of the *chizuk* I was trying to give him. That week the *parsha* was the *parsha* of *shidduchim*, *Chayei*

Sarah. Eliezer is sent to find a wife for Yitzchak and davens to *Hashem* that he will be successful. Rivkah comes along and lives up to all the tests that Eliezer had set up as a sign that she is poised to become the wife of Yitzchak.

והאיש משתאה לה מחריש לדעת ההצליח יקוק דרכו אם־לא⁷

The man was astounded and thought silently whether Hashem has made his pursuit successful or not.

Eliezer wanted to know if he was successful in his mission. Why does the *pasuk* tell us he wanted to see if he was successful or not? Every word and every letter in the holy Torah is precious and necessary. There are entire *halachos* learned from one extra letter. Shouldn't the Torah have just said he wanted to see if he was successful? The obvious other possibility would be that he was not successful. If stating one wants to see if he will be successful, there is no need to state "or not," as that is already clear and understood.

Harav Spiegel suggested that the Torah is enlightening us that when it comes to *shidduchim* if there is success there is great *simcha*. If there is not success there is also great *simcha*, as one does not want to end up with a spouse not perfect for you. Therefore the Torah emphasizes "or not" as that also calls for a *mazel tov*.

Motzei Shabbos, immediately after making *havdallah*, I ran to the phone to call my *talmid* who I knew would appreciate this Torah. It was truly the exact antidote to what he was feeling. As I hoped, he took much inspiration from the Torah, but not close to as much inspiration as I received from the events that followed.

He eventually found out why that girl decided to end the

---

7. *Parshas Chayei Sarah, perek* 24, *pasuk* 21.

relationship. Although she as well felt like things were progressing nicely, she thought he was perfect for a close friend of hers. She could not continue with that thought in her mind. She broke up in order to set him up with her friend. Today, my *talmid* is married to that close friend and has a beautiful family and a house of *shalom bayis*.

"Or not!" We must realize *Hashem* is always with us and bringing us what is best. In this particular story the "or not" literally lead to the *mazel tov*. *Beshaa tova umutzlachas* to all who are in need of a *shidduch*. *Bezras Hashem* the right person at the right time!!

Parshas Vayigash

To Cling to a Rebbi

ויאמר יוסף אל־אחיו אני יוסף העוד אבי חי ולא־יכלו אחיו לענות
אתו כי נבהלו מפניו[1]

Yosef said to his brothers, "I am Yosef is my father still alive."
The brothers were unable to answer as they were flustered in
front of him.

ONE OF THE MOST special relationships influencing one's
spirituality as well as emotional well being is one's bond with a
Rebbe. Not merely as a Rebbi to learn Torah and *halacha* from,
but also to have as a role model in how to maneuver through
this sometimes difficult world – a Rebbi to have by one's side
in the best of times and the worst of times. A Rebbi that one
knows is always keeping an eye on him to keep one from stray-
ing from *emes*. It is the relationship of a father to a son, and the
bond of a best friend molded into one.

In my humble eyes there is no more emotional *Parsha* in the
Torah than *Parshas Vayigash*. My Bubby would always share
with me that it was her favorite Parsha in the Torah. Who is
not brought to tears yearly when listening to the Torah reading

---

1. *Parshas Vayigosh, perek 45, pasuk 3.*

of Yosef revealing himself to his brothers, and the pinnacle of Yosef and Yaakov meeting for the first time in 22 years?

After wiping away the tears of this emotional moment, one realizes that the first words Yosef chooses to share with his brothers are puzzling in many ways. After revealing himself he immediately asks if his father is still alive. To anyone following the story line until this point this inquiry is unintelligible. Immediately preceding that statement, Yehuda argues to Yosef that if Binyomin was left in *Mitzrayim* their father would not be able to handle the loss. Yosef was well aware prior to this question that his father was alive and well. Why was he at this point asking about the welfare of his father? If one continues to read the subsequent *pasukim* we find no answer to this question. Why is it that the brothers felt no need to respond? Additionally, why does Yosef refer to his father in a possessive singular tense, my father, is Yaakov not the father of all the brothers?

The Slonimer Rebbe in his classic work the *Nesivos Shalom* uses an idea that he develops often in his *seforim* to explain the inquiry of Yosef.[2] *Tzaddikim* are on a lifelong mission to make every vestige of their body as holy as possible. *Tzaddikim* strive to make their body holy and pure until it will serve *Hashem* unconsciously. Even if there are times when the *Tzaddik* would be unaware of how to act, his holy body will act appropriately. One example of this would be the much discussed act of Moshe hitting the rock. How could it be that the greatest leader of *Bnei Yisrael* could disobey the word of *Hashem*? The *Nesivos Shalom*[3] bases his explanation on the *Ohr Hachaim*[4] that states that if

---

2. *Nesivos Shalom, Parshas Vayigosh, "Haod Avi Chai".*
3. *Nesivos Shalom, Parshas Bereishis, "Cheit Haadamah".*
4. *Ohr Hacahaim, Vaeschanan, perek 3, pasuk 25,* based on *Sotah 9a.*

Moshe would have been able to enter *Eretz Yisrael* and build the *Beis Hamikdash* it would have been a building impossible to ever destroy. The *Beis Hamikdash* built by the hand of Moshe would posses such a high level of holiness that it would be indestructible. When *Bnei Yisrael* would eventually falter and need to be punished, *Hashem* would not have been able to take out His wrath on the *Beis Hamikdash* and would have had to destroy the Jewish nation. Although Moshe was unaware of this in his conscious state, his body was so pure that it knew what it needed to do. The hand of Moshe understood that *Hashem* wanted it to hit the rock so that Moshe could be punished and not enter *Eretz Yisrael*. This seemingly wrong act would lead to the salvation of *Bnei Yisrael*. A *tzaddik* purifies his body to the extent that it knows to only follow the will of *Hashem*.

Yaakov *Avinu* was another *Tzaddik* that was able to reach such a level. The *pasuk*[5] teaches us that Yaakov refused to be consoled after being led to believe Yosef had perished. Does this not seem like a lacking in *emunah*? Shouldn't a *tzaddik* be able to say *Baruch Dayan Emes* as we find by Aharon[6] after the death of his two sons? How could it be that Yaakov refused to be comforted for 22 years?

Yaakov, in his subconscious, understood that Yosef was alive and he needed to never forget him. His body knew that it needed to think of Yosef and not leave that bond. For Yosef to survive alone in a society of immorality and impurity he needed to always be connected to his father and Rebbi. Although on the surface Yaakov was unaware of Yosef's whereabouts, he had made his body into one full of purity always

---

5. *Parshas Vayeishev, perek* 38, *pasuk* 35.
6. *Parshas Shemini, perek* 10, *pasuk* 3.

following the desires of *Hashem*. He knew deep down that he could not move on.

In *Parshas Vayeishev*, when being seduced by the wife of Potiphar, we are able to witness the importance of this bond being carried out. One can not imagine how difficult that test must have been for Yosef. Somehow Yosef is successful and able to run from the temptation. Rashi[7] teaches, based on a *gemara* in *Sotah*, how it was that Yosef was able overcome that challenge. At that very moment he saw the image of his father. He was connected to his father and Rebbi always, and therefore would not fall.

What was the depth behind the image of his father protecting him? If one adds up the *gematria* of *lev deyokno shel aviv*, at the heart of the image of his father, the numerical value is 577. This is the exact *gematria* of *assei Rav*, make for yourself a Rebbi. One must always be bound to a Rebbi who will provide the spiritual sustenance to succeed.

Now we can understand those first words shared by Yosef with his brothers. After revealing himself to his brothers, Yosef wanted to assure his family that he was still spiritually strong as well. He understood that to his family, physical existence is meaningless if he was spiritually dead. He therefore explained to his brothers that he was the same *eved Hashem*. He explained this to them by telling them "My father is still alive." This was not a question, but a statement. Yosef was telling his brothers that his father and rebbi is still alive within him and he is still connected to him and that is what kept him spiritually alive. Yosef was not asking about his father's health or expecting a response. Yosef was revealing the secret of his personal success!!

---

7. *Parshas Vayeishev, perek* 39, *pasuk* 11.

A bond with a Rebbi is a foundation for success during one's spiritual road of life.

This was also the message that Yosef was conveying to Yaakov when sending him the wagons. *Rashi,*[8] quoting the Midrash, teaches how Yosef was relaying to Yaakov that he had not forgotten the last Torah they learned together. Yosef wanted Yaakov to immediately know that he was spiritually alive. The final Torah they learned together before Yosef's disappearance was that of *eglah arufah*. They learned about the case of a calf whose neck was broken in the event of an unsolved murder. The root word in Hebrew for calf and wagon are the same, *eglah*, and therefore the wagons sent to Yaakov assured his father that he had not forgotten the holy Torah that he was taught.

Is there a deeper message to be found in this particular Torah of *eglah arufah* being hinted to by Yosef? Of course this was the final Torah that was learned, but is there a reason that *Hashem* made sure that this was the final Torah between father and son, between Rebbi and *talmid*?

The *gemara* in *Sotah*[9] explains that when a murdered individual is found, the *tzaddikim* of the closest city are held responsible. The righteous people should have escorted the person out of their city, and therefore their hands carry the blood of the murdered. If this person would have have been accompanied by another, surely he would still be alive.

Yosef was again telling Yaakov and his brothers that I am still alive because I was never alone. I was escorted spiritually every moment by my father and Rebbi. I am still alive today because of that bond and connection. When one is connected to a Rebbi one has the lifeline to succeed in all situations.

---

8. *Parshas Vayigosh, perek* 46, *pasuk* 27.
9. *Sotah* 46b.

I once heard from Rav Avraham Shorr in the name of the *Bnei Yisachar* that the *mabul* occurred in the year 1,656. This was obviously the lowest point in the existence of the world. Mankind sank so low spiritually that the whole world needed to be uprooted and rebuilt. The *gemara* in *Succah*[10] explains, based on *pasukim*, that the *yetzer hara* has seven different names. If one adds up the *gematria* of all seven names the numerical value is exactly 1,656. The generation of the flood was taken over by all the powers of the *yetzer hara*, and therefore needed to be destroyed.

How does one defeat all seven levels of the *yetzer hara*? How do we ensure that we do not fall to the levels of the generation of the *mabul* again? We must always be connected to *Rabbeim* guiding our lives. If we trust ourselves alone, we will surely fall. If one adds up the *millui* of the name Moshe, the numerical value is also exactly 1,656. Moshe was our greatest of *Rabbeim*. He was the Rebbi of *Bnei Yisrael*. This is the *koach* needed to defeat the *yetzer hara*. Not just when in yeshiva, but our entire lives we must be bound to our *Rabbeim*. A Rebbi must be by one's side for advice, halachic guidance, and most importantly a protection from falling prey to the *yetzer hara* looming around every corner.

*

The following story is an example of how a Rebbi is always by our side.

As I mentioned in the story for *Parshas Vayeishev*, in 2008 I had the privilege to be in Meiron for *Lag B'omer*. On that year *Lag B'omer* was on a Thursday night and Friday and therefore the celebration usually spread over 2 nights was packed into

---

10. *Succah* 52a.

one. The many *tzaddikim* that visit therefore all came to visit Rav Shimon *ztz"l* on this night. Among the *tzaddikim* present was Harav Tzvi Meyer Zyllberberg *Shlita*.To watch the *simchas hachaim* as Rav Tzvi Meyer danced with his holy demeanor was a sight imprinted on my heart.

At one point I was standing outside the *kever* and saw a crowd of people quickly coming my way. I immediately saw that Rav Tzvi Meyer was in the front leaving the *kever* followed by about 100 *chasidim*. As the *tzaddik* moved close to where I was standing a man holding his three year old son ran in front of Rav Tzvi Meyer and handed the *tzaddik* a pair of scissors to take the first cut for his son's *upsherin*. (One of the special *minhagim* on *Lag B'omer* is to give *upsherins* and initiate the *chinuch* of those boys who turned three during the days of *sefiras ha-omer* when they could not cut their hair.) The *chassidim* quickly surround the *tzaddik* to try and get a good view of the cutting. At this point I took my camera and held it over the huddle of *chassidim* to hopefully get a nice shot of the *tzaddik's* cutting. *Baruch Hashem* I was able to take a beautiful picture.

The father of the young boy excitedly came over to me to ask if I got a good picture. He explained everything happened so quickly that he had no time to take a picture himself and was so happy that someone captured this special moment. He told me that Rav Tzvi Meir was his Rebbi and he would love to receive a copy of the picture. After talking for a few more moments I found out that he was a Rebbi in Yeshivas Ohr Somayach in Yerushalayim. At the time my cousin Betzalel was learning in Ohr Somayach and of course I immediately realized that I was talking to my cousin's Rebbe. I was easily able to make a copy of the picture and send it to Rabbi Levine with my cousin.

Only on *Lag B'omer* in Meiron do moments such as these seem natural and not miraculous.

At that special moment in that special place and at that special time, Rabbi Levine's Rebbe was at his side to begin the chinuch of his son. Rabbi Levine, until today, continues to guide my cousin as a Rebbe who is always by his side as well.

Parshas Vayechi

To Live a Life of Simcha

וירא יוסף לאפרים בני שלשים גם בני מכיר בן־מנשה ילדו על־ברכי
יוסף[1]

*Yosef saw the children of a third generation from Ephrayim.
The children of Machir the son of Menashe was also raised on
the knees of Yosef.*

ALTHOUGH I HAVE THUS FAR always ended the Torah
for each *parsha* with a story, I must add an introductory story
to this final *parsha* in *Sefer Breishis* in addition to the one with
which I will conclude.

I want to write about being *besimcha,* as I believe feeling
happy is the foundation to all growth and productivity. The
very first idea that I thought of which linked the concept of
happiness and *Parshas Vayechi* was from the Chasam Sofer.
When I reviewed the Chasam Sofer prior to writing this, I
found that the Chasam Sofer began his idea talking about a
Bar Mitzvah. I was truly amazed. The driving force that gave
me the inspiration to finally record Torah in a *sefer* was my son
Shmuel's upcoming *Bar Mitzvah.* I decided that in honor of the

---

1. *Parshas Vayechi, perek* 50, *pasuk* 23.

Bar Mitzvah of my *bechor* I was going to bring some concrete *ruchnius* into this world to help instill in Shmuel guidance for life. It was therefore truly amazing that for the final Torah of the *sefer,* I chanced upon a Torah discussing one's *bar mitzvah.* Of course nothing is by chance so here is the Torah the One Above brought me.

There is nothing more desired in our journey of life, whether consciously or unconsciously, than happiness. Some believe they will find it in a trophy wife, others in luxurious wealth, while others in the thoughtless moment of a pill, bottle or cloud of smoke. As Rav Pam, who my son Shmuel Yaakov is named after, would often say, "We all search for the city of happiness, but don't realize that it is found in a state of mind." Rav Pam's words can be sourced in the fact that the letters for *besimcha* are the same letters as *machshava* – thought. True *simcha* is found in the understanding of the importance of the connection to a meaningful and productive life. True *simcha* can only be found in a life of closeness to *Hashem* which brings a feeling of completeness, consistently and eternally.

In the *pasuk* quoted above we find that Yosef lived to enjoy three generations of offspring. Although this is a very nice fact to know, our holy Torah does not add detail for the reader's pleasure. What is the significance of Yosef living to see his great grandchildren?

The Magen Avraham[2] explains that when a boy becomes a bar mitzvah there is a mitzvah to prepare a *seudah* in celebration. The Chasam Sofer[3] explains that the mother of the boy is the one who is responsible for making this *seudah* and not the father. Besides for the fact that in reality a mother is

---

2. *Siman* 225, *Seif Katan* 4.
3. *Chasam Sofer Al Hatorah, Parshas Vayechi,* p. 246.

generally more responsible in planning this special event, why does this obligation fall on the mother more than the father? The Chasam Sofer explains that until now the father had a mitzvah to educate his son in the *mitzvos* of *Hashem*. This *mitzvah* of *chinuch* ends with this boy becoming a young man as he passes the age of thirteen. The loss of this mitzvah brings some sadness to the father and therefore, although full of joy for his son, the happiness is not complete. It is therefore the mother who is asked to plan this event with a heart full of joy.

The mitzvah of *chinuch* is not merely for one's children, but for one's grandchildren and great grandchildren as well. The Midrash explains that only until the third generation of offspring does one worry about their welfare. The Chasam Sofer learns from here that one is only responsible to educate the first three generation of progeny. This is the lesson the Torah was teaching when speaking of Yosef's connection to three generations. The Torah was describing the full life that Yosef was privileged to live, as he would not feel closely connected to any generation beyond the third.

The Chasam Sofer then brilliantly suggests that at the moment that the father loses his *mitzvah* of *chinuch*, at that very same instant, the *bar mitzvah* boy gains the yoke of *mitzvos*. How so? Because the very first *mitzvah* that this young man can fulfill is not *krias shemah*, as is commonly quoted, but rather to be *besimcha* and rejoice in the privilege he has to accept the *mitzvos* of *Hashem*. This *simcha* is a fulfillment of the *mitzvah Mideoraisa* to serve *Hashem* with a joyous heart. One is obligated to try to always be happy. This *mitzvah* is the very first *mitzvah* with which one begins his adult life as a servant of *Hashem*.

Rabbeinu Bachayei[4] explains that the source for the *mitzvah*

---

4. *Parshas Ki Savo, perek 28, pasuk 47.*

of being *besimcha* in the Torah is found in *Parshas Ki Savo*. After listing all the calamities that can befall *Bnei Yisrael*, the Torah teaches us the reason behind these tragedies.

תחת אשר לא־עבדת את־יקוק א־להיך בשמחה ובטוב לבב מרב כל⁵

Because you didn't serve Hashem out of joy with a good heart based on everything else going on.

The simple understanding of this *pasuk* is that because we were not happy *Hashem* will bring us the curses of the *tochacha*. Happiness is a *mitzvah* that shows *Hashem* that we are one with Him and feel His presence. A lack of *simcha* is not merely a failure of the observance of a single *mitzvah*, but a sign that one's total connection to *Hashem* is incomplete. Rav Aharon of Karlin⁶ would say "Sadness is not an *aveira*, but brings one to the worst of *aveiros*, and happiness is not a *mitzvah*, but brings one to the highest of places."

The Tanya⁷ goes so far as to call a person who is not *besimcha* a non believer. When one truly believes that *Hashem* is by one's side, one feels a constant sense of calm and contentment. This is not to say one is not permitted to experience sadness and frustration. We are all human and experience life in the raw moments in which we find ourselves. At the same time, however, there is no place for depression and deep sadness, for one who is connected to *Hashem* is living a meaningful and productive life. Even at times of sadness there is a sense of *simcha* in one's heart knowing that *Hashem* is by our side.

The Arizal would say that whatever he achieved in life was in return for his *simcha* stemming from *avodas Hashem*.⁸

5. Ibid.
6. *Shevili Pinchas*, 5772, *Parshas Ki Savo*.
7. *Igros Hakodesh* 11.
8. *Shevilei Pinchas*, 5772, *Parshas Ki Savo*.

Rav Menachem Mendel of Kotzk has a beautiful teaching on the following famous Gemara.

> אמר רב יהודה בריה דרב שמואל בר שילת משמיה דרב: כשם
> שמשנכנס אב ממעטין בשמחה – כך משנכנס אדר מרבין בשמחה[9]
> *Rav Yehudah the son of Rav Shmuel the son of Shilos says in the name of Rav, "Just as when we enter into the month of Av we must decrease our joy, so too when we enter into Adar we must increase our joy."*

By analyzing this *gemara* a *Yid* extrapolates that one must always be *besimcha*. When Adar enters we are not told to begin to be happy, but to increase our joy. We can only increase something which we already have. When Av enters and heralds the time designated to commemorate Jewish tragedies throughout history, we decrease our joy. We only decrease, but do not completely rid ourselves of all *simcha*. We learn from here that we must always be happy. There are times when we increase and times when we decrease, but a Jew must always be happy.

Bezras Hashem my son Shmuel should be *zoche* to fulfill this first *mitzvah* with full appreciation of its importance. This will be the start of a life of *simcha* in *avodas Hashem*.

*

The following story is about a *Yid* who is clearly living a life of *simcha*.

As I mentioned in the story of *Parshas Toldos*, over the past few years, with the help of a very special friend and the devotion of my *Eishes Chayil*, I have been *zoche* to spend the holiest day of the year steps from the *makom* of the *Avodah* of the day, davening with my holy *talmidim* in Yeshivas Netiv Aryeh. Words can not do justice to describe the beautiful *teffilos* or

---

9. *Taanis* 29a.

the feeling of being able to look up and see *Har Habayis* while reading the *avodah* of the *Kohen Gadol* on that very spot.

A few years ago, Yom Kippur fell out on a Thursday and I was therefore able to stay for the following *Shabbos kodesh*. On *Leil Shabbos,* after a beautiful *seudah* at the home of Harav Yoel Rackovsky, I was able to share in the *shalom zachor* of the birth of a first son to my friend Josh Shapiro. By the time it was over it was close to 1:00 am and I was about to return to my hotel to go to sleep. Being my last night in the holy land, however, I changed my mind and decided to walk with a few *talmidim* including Eli Pollak and Jonny Fruchter to the *Kosel* to spend time steeped in *teffilah*, song and introspection.

When we arrived at the holy wall there were about five other *Yidden* there connecting to *Hashem*. I sat at a *shtender* and began to daven and think. Suddenly I noticed a Breslover *chassid* who was dancing in a circle and singing all by himself right in front of the *Kossel*. I could sense there was something very holy about this *Yid* who was full of *simcha* and I wanted to feel it as well. I got up and walked right up to the wall a couple feet in front of him pretending to *daven*, but in reality was just absorbing his *kedusha*. At this point another *Yid* at the *Kossel* decided to join the *chassid* in his *tantz*. Once he did, my five *talmidim* and I, along with the other five individuals at the *Kossel* all joined in one circle of *ruchnius*. There we were, at 2:00 am on a *Leil Shabbos* at the *Kossel*. Every one of us felt the moment in a way that words fail to capture. Our dress, appearance or affiliation had no bearings at that moment. We were just a few *Yidden*, singing and dancing with the *Ribbono Shel Olam* in the middle. This portrayal of *simcha* continued for about 20 minutes. When the dance finally ended, we all said *Gut Shabbos* to each other and went our own ways with very few words exchanged, but all of our hearts were united as one.

About 4 months later I was *zoche* to return to *Eretz Yisrael* to spend a week with my special *talmidim* learning in *Yeshivos* throughout our country. After a long day with *talmidim*, at about 2:00 am, I finally made my way to the *Kossel* for the first time that trip. As I walk down the ramp and approach the *Kossel* plaza, an unfamiliar *chassid* approached me with a huge smile. He gave me a big *shalom* and asked if I remembered him. I unfortunately had no idea who he was. He then said to me, "*Harikud, Leil Shabbat*" "The dance, on *Shabbos* night!" I immediately understood that *Hashem* brought me back together with the Holy Breslover *chassid* who of course was named Nachman. We spontaneously started to dance, singing the same song we sang together on that amazing Friday night.

This only happens in the holy city by the holy wall with the holy people. Two nights in a row at the *Kossel* with a 4 month break in between. Trust me when I say every single one of us who were *zoche* to be there that night have never stopped *tantzing* and have never stopped feeling the *simcha*.

Just as a lacking of *simcha* brings all the tragedies of the *tochacha*, being *besimcha* can bring the long awaited *geulah*. *Hashem* wants so badly for us to be happy, as any parent wants his children to always be happy. A very special woman once taught me that a parent is only as happy as their saddest child. Lets us bring the *geulah* together *besimcha*.

Of course the *gematria* for *Hasimcha*, the simcha that we all should have, is 358. This is the exact *gematria* as *Mashiach!!*

About the Author

Rabbi ARYEH COHEN learned in Yeshivas Kerem B'Yavneh, Yeshiva University, Lander's Beis Medrash LeTalmud, where he received his *semicha*, and Yeshivas Mir Yerushalayim, where he forged a special relationship with R. Nosson Tzvi Finkel, *ztz"l*. He has taught young men and women in DRS Yeshiva High school, as well as SKA and NCSY Kollel Summer programs. After serving as a 12th grade Rebbe in DRS for the past 10 years, he now also serves as the *Mashgiach Ruchani* of the Yeshiva. He is well known for his unique combination of penchant Torah thoughts and analytic learning style, coupled with his warm and enthusiastic *shiurim* in which he seamlessly weaves classic *meforshim* and *mussar* ideas with *chassidus, machshava* and *gematrias*. One cannot help but be inspired after walking away from one of his *shiurim,* as his heart is felt in every thought. He has mentored hundreds of *talmidim* during their high school and post-high school years, who remain closely connected to their Rebbe. Whether at his Thursday night *shiur* for alumni in his home, his *shalosh seudos* meals and *tishin* with scores of talmidim, purim *seudas*, late night *slichos* at the Ohel of the Lubavitcher Rebbe, trips to *kivrei tzadikim* in Europe, or dancing at the *Kosel* until the early morning hours, he is beloved by his talmidim for his sincerity and for the lifelong bonds he forges with them. He resides in Cedarhurst, N.Y. with his wife Shaindy, and five children.

To contact Rabbi Cohen email: rabbiaryehcohen@gmail.com.